Investing In ETFs

The Roadmap To Portfolio Success

Nathan Venture, D

Although the author and publisher have made every effort to ensure that the information in this book was correct at press time, the author and publisher do not assume and hereby disclaim any liability to any party for any loss, damage, or disruption caused by errors or omissions, whether such errors or omissions result from negligence, accident, or any other cause.

This publication is designed to provide accurate and authoritative information with regard to the subject matter covered. It is sold with the understanding that the publisher is not engaged in rendering professional services. If legal advice or other expert assistance is required, the services of a competent professional should be sought.

The fact that an organization or website is referred to in this work as a citation and/or a potential source of further information does not mean that the author or the publisher endorses the information the organization or website may provide or recommendations it may make.

Please remember that Internet websites listed in this work may have changed or disappeared between when this work was written and when it is read.

Contents

Introduction

Investing in ETFs begins with a simple but important recognition: the fund you choose is not just a ticker symbol, but a set of design choices that determine how your capital is deployed, how closely the fund follows its stated objective, and how it behaves under different market conditions. Two ETFs can appear similar on the surface and still differ meaningfully in index construction, turnover, trading liquidity, holdings transparency, and tax treatment. Those differences matter because they affect cost, risk, and the role the fund can realistically play in a portfolio.

Another reason ETFs deserve careful study is that their rise has changed the structure of investing itself. Passive funds now direct enormous capital flows and hold significant stakes across public markets [2]. That scale gives ETFs practical advantages for investors, but it also means that understanding their mechanics is no longer optional. When a product is widely used, small differences in structure and execution can have large consequences over time.

The ETF market also reflects a broader shift toward transparency and rules-based investing. Investors are increasingly expected to evaluate not only performance, but the process behind performance: what the fund owns, how it selects those holdings, how often it trades, and what assumptions are embedded in the index or strategy. Disclosure plays a central role in that evaluation because it helps investors compare products and place appropriate confidence in what they are buying [4].

At the same time, ETF investing is not a substitute for judgment. The availability of low-cost, liquid funds can make portfolio construction easier, but it can also encourage overconfidence, excessive trading, or shallow product selection. The best results usually come from treating ETFs as building blocks within a disciplined process rather than as shortcuts to market success. That means asking basic questions before buying: What exposure does this fund actually provide? How concentrated is it? What costs are visible, and what costs are hidden in trading and implementation? How well does it fit the rest of the portfolio?

These questions become especially important because not all diversification is real diversification. A portfolio can contain many funds and still be heavily exposed to the same industries, factors, or market risks. Likewise, a low expense ratio does not guarantee a good outcome if the ETF is difficult to trade, poorly constructed, or too narrow for the investor's objectives. The point is not to avoid complexity entirely, but to understand where complexity adds value and where it merely adds noise.

For that reason, ETF investing rewards a methodical approach. The reader who understands structure, selection, portfolio fit, and risk control will be better positioned to use ETFs as intended: as efficient tools for building and maintaining an investment plan. The chapters ahead focus on those decisions in sequence, beginning with what ETFs are, why they matter, and how they differ from other common investment vehicles.

CHAPTER 1

Chapter 1: Why ETFs Matter in Modern Investing

Before an investor can evaluate an ETF intelligently, it helps to understand why this vehicle has become such a central part of modern portfolios. ETFs sit at the intersection of fund investing and market trading, which gives them a structure that is familiar in some respects and distinct in others. That hybrid design has reshaped how individuals, advisers, and institutions build portfolios, and it has also changed the way benchmarks, implementation, and product selection are discussed in practice [11][15]. The sections that follow focus on the basic mechanics and the key distinctions that matter most at the outset, so the reader can approach ETF choices with a clearer framework rather than treating every fund as interchangeable.

What an ETF is and how it works in the market

An ETF, or exchange-traded fund, is a pooled investment vehicle that holds a basket of assets and issues shares that trade on an exchange like a stock. That basic structure is what gives an ETF its hybrid character: it is a fund because it provides exposure to many underlying securities through one purchase, but it is traded because investors can buy and sell its shares throughout the market session rather than waiting for end-of-day pricing. The result is a product designed to make broad market access, targeted exposure, and portfolio implementation more efficient.

What the investor actually owns is not the underlying stocks, bonds, or other assets directly, but shares in the fund that represent an interest in that portfolio. The fund itself is managed to follow a stated objective, which may be as simple as tracking a broad index or as specific as focusing on a sector, country, style, or strategy. Because the ETF is built around a rules-based portfolio or active management process, its market behavior is shaped by both the composition of the holdings and the way those holdings are packaged into shares. This is why two ETFs that seem similar by name can behave differently in practice.

The market price of an ETF is determined by supply and demand during trading hours, just as with a stock. However, that price is anchored by the value of the underlying portfolio, commonly expressed as net asset value, or NAV. When the market price drifts too far above or below the value of the holdings, a creation and redemption mechanism helps bring it back in line. Large institutional participants known as authorized participants can assemble or deliver the basket of underlying assets in exchange for ETF shares, or do the reverse. This mechanism is central to the ETF structure because it helps support liquidity and keeps the trading price close to the value of the fund's assets.

That process matters because it means ETF liquidity is not the same thing as the trading volume printed on a screen. A fund with modest daily volume may still be relatively easy to trade if the underlying market is deep and the creation-redemption process is functioning normally. Conversely, a fund that appears active may still be expensive to trade if the underlying holdings are hard to price, less liquid, or concentrated in a narrow segment of the market. For this reason, the ETF share market and the market for the underlying securities work together, and the second is often just as important as the first.

In practical terms, an ETF gives investors a way to express a view, build a diversified allocation, or manage cash with a single trade. A broad market ETF can serve as a core equity holding, while a bond ETF can provide interest-rate or credit exposure without requiring the investor to buy individual bonds. Sector, country, and thematic ETFs make it possible to target specific areas of the market with precision. This flexibility is one reason passive investing has become so influential in capital markets, with ETFs and index funds now directing enormous flows and holding substantial ownership stakes across public companies [2].

The market role of ETFs has also expanded beyond simple indexing. Some funds are designed around environmental, social, and governance screens or other label-based criteria, which means the ETF can influence not only portfolio construction but also how capital is allocated across industries and issuers. Research on green finance and ESG index design shows that disclosure, index construction, and provider standards can materially shape what qualifies for inclusion and how capital is directed [4][21]. In that sense, an ETF is not just a trading instrument; it is also an allocation mechanism that can transmit investor preferences into the market structure itself.

Because the ETF is both a fund and a security, its behavior reflects multiple layers at once: the quality of the underlying holdings, the rules of the index or strategy, the efficiency of the creation-redemption process, and the conditions in the secondary market. That combination is what makes ETFs useful, but it is also what makes them worth understanding carefully. The ticker symbol tells only part of the story. To know what an ETF is doing in the market, an investor has to look at what it holds, how it is built, and how it trades.

How ETFs differ from mutual funds, stocks, and index funds

An ETF is often compared with a mutual fund because both provide diversified exposure through a pooled vehicle, but the way they are bought, sold, and used in a portfolio is different. A mutual fund is generally priced once per day at its net asset value, and orders are executed after the market closes. An ETF, by contrast, trades throughout the day on an exchange, so its price moves as supply and demand change in real time. That trading feature gives ETFs flexibility, but it also means the investor must pay attention to bid-ask spreads, order types, and intraday price behavior in a way that mutual fund investors usually do not.

The difference in trading mechanics leads to a difference in the investor experience. With a mutual fund, the focus is often on the fund's strategy, expense ratio, and end-of-day pricing. With an ETF, the focus expands to include market liquidity and execution quality. A highly liquid ETF may trade with very tight spreads, while a less liquid one may still be perfectly usable but require more care when placing orders. This is one reason ETFs are sometimes described as a fund wrapped in a market instrument: the portfolio exposure is familiar, but the trading process is closer to that of a stock.

ETFs also differ from stocks in a fundamental way. A stock represents ownership in a single company, so its return depends heavily on the fortunes of that one issuer. An ETF usually holds many securities, which spreads company-specific risk across a basket of holdings. That diversification is one of the main reasons investors use ETFs in the first place. At the same time, an ETF share itself is still a security that trades like a stock, which can create confusion. An investor buying shares of a broad market ETF is not buying a business in the operating sense; the investor is buying a claim on a portfolio of assets designed to track a stated objective.

This distinction matters because the risks are different. A stock can rise or fall based on earnings, management decisions, product launches, or litigation involving one firm. An ETF's value is driven by the combined movement of its underlying holdings and by the rules of the index or strategy it follows. Even when an ETF is concentrated in one sector or theme, it is still not the same as owning a single stock, because the fund structure introduces diversification, rebalancing, and portfolio-level rules that individual shares do not have. Passive funds, including ETFs and index funds, have become major holders of corporate equities and an increasingly important force in capital markets [2].

The comparison with index funds is more subtle, because an ETF can be an index fund, but not all index funds are ETFs. The term index fund describes a strategy: a fund that seeks to track a benchmark rather than try to outperform it through security selection. That strategy can be delivered through a mutual fund structure or through an ETF structure. In other words, "index fund" tells you how the portfolio is managed, while "ETF" tells you how the shares trade. Many investors use the terms interchangeably, but they are not synonyms. A low-cost S&P 500 ETF and a low-cost S&P 500 index mutual fund may pursue nearly identical exposures while differing in trading access, settlement, tax behavior, and the way investors interact with them.

Because of that distinction, the real comparison is often not ETF versus index fund, but ETF versus index mutual fund. Both may be passive, rules-based, and benchmark-oriented. Both may offer broad diversification and low operating expenses. Yet an ETF can usually be bought or sold intraday, used more easily in tactical allocation, and integrated into accounts where trading flexibility matters. A mutual fund may be more convenient for automatic purchases, dollar-cost averaging, or investors who prefer end-of-day pricing and do not want to think about spreads. The structure does not determine whether the portfolio is active or passive; it determines how the investment is accessed and transacted.

This is also why an ETF can be used for strategies that resemble mutual fund investing, but with different operational consequences. An investor can hold a broad market ETF for years as a core position, just as one might hold an index mutual fund. Or the same ETF can be traded more actively around cash flows, rebalancing, or short-term views. That flexibility is part of the appeal, but it should not obscure the underlying discipline required. The more an investor treats an ETF like a stock in terms of trading, the more important execution becomes. The more an investor treats it like a fund in terms of long-term allocation, the more important benchmark fit and portfolio role become.

In practice, the key question is not which wrapper is "better" in the abstract. It is which structure matches the investor's purpose. Stocks provide concentrated ownership in individual companies. Mutual funds offer pooled exposure with end-of-day pricing and often simpler automatic investing. Index funds describe a passive management approach that can live inside either wrapper. ETFs combine fund diversification with exchange trading, which makes them especially useful when liquidity, flexibility, and tax-aware implementation matter. That hybrid character is what gives ETFs their distinct place in modern portfolios, and it is also why they must be evaluated on both their investment design and their market behavior.

The main advantages of ETFs: low costs, liquidity, and diversification

The first advantage most investors notice is cost. ETFs are typically built to track an index or a clearly defined strategy without the heavy operating structure that often accompanies more complex fund arrangements. That usually translates into lower expense ratios, and over long horizons even small annual differences can compound into meaningful savings. The benefit is not limited to the published fee alone. Because many ETFs are designed to be rules-based and relatively low-turnover, they may also generate fewer internal trading costs than more actively managed vehicles. In practice, this means more of the portfolio's return can stay with the investor rather than being absorbed by ongoing fund expenses.

Low cost matters because it creates a more favorable starting point for performance. An ETF does not need to outperform by a large margin to be useful; it simply needs to deliver the intended market exposure efficiently. That efficiency is one reason passive and index-linked funds have become so influential in modern portfolio construction. Research on fund design and benchmark usage has shown that the details of index selection and implementation can vary widely, which is one reason investors should not assume all low-cost products are identical [10]. Even so, when two funds offer similar exposure, the lower-cost structure is often the more attractive option because fees, trading costs, and tracking differences all affect the investor's realized outcome.

Liquidity is the second major advantage, and it is one of the features that separates ETFs from many traditional pooled investments. Because ETF shares trade on an exchange during market hours, investors can buy or sell them at prices that update throughout the day. This flexibility is useful for rebalancing, cash deployment, and responding to changing portfolio needs. It also allows investors to use familiar order types, such as limit orders, to exert more control over execution. For many portfolios, that intraday tradability makes ETFs easier to incorporate than vehicles that price only once at the end of the day.

Liquidity, however, should be understood carefully. An ETF's trading activity in the market is not the same thing as the liquidity of every underlying security it holds. Some funds trade heavily and have narrow bid-ask spreads, while others may appear quiet on the exchange but still be able to create and redeem shares efficiently because the underlying market is deep. This distinction matters because investors often focus only on the ticker's volume and overlook the broader market structure supporting the fund. In other words, ETF liquidity is a combination of share trading, creation and redemption activity, and the liquidity of the portfolio itself. When those elements are healthy, the investor usually benefits from smoother execution and tighter trading costs.

Diversification is the third core advantage, and for many investors it is the most important one. A single ETF can provide exposure to dozens, hundreds, or even thousands of securities, which helps reduce the impact of any one company or issuer on the portfolio. That broad exposure can be especially valuable for investors who want to build a portfolio without having to select individual stocks or bonds one by one. Instead of relying on a few concentrated positions, the investor can obtain a more balanced representation of a market, sector, region, or asset class through one trade.

The diversification benefit is not just about owning more securities; it is about spreading risk across different sources of return. A broad U.S. equity ETF, for example, can reduce company-specific risk relative to holding a small number of stocks. A bond ETF can add a different return pattern than equities. International ETFs can reduce dependence on a single economy or currency area. Studies of capital flows and benchmark behavior also show that many investors and institutions use ETFs as building blocks for larger allocation decisions, which reinforces their role as efficient tools for diversification across markets and geographies [25].

At the same time, diversification does not eliminate risk. If an ETF is highly concentrated in one sector, one country, or one factor style, it may still behave like a focused bet rather than a broadly diversified holding.

These three advantages reinforce one another. Low costs help preserve returns, liquidity helps investors implement decisions efficiently, and diversification helps manage portfolio risk. Together, they explain why ETFs are often used as core holdings rather than as temporary trading instruments. They can serve both purposes, but their real strength is that they make it possible to build a portfolio that is efficient, tradable, and broadly exposed without requiring excessive complexity. That combination is difficult to replicate with many other investment vehicles, especially for investors who want disciplined exposure to markets without paying a premium for convenience.

Common misconceptions and limitations investors should understand

One common misconception is that an ETF is automatically a simple, low-risk shortcut to diversification. In reality, an ETF is only a wrapper. What matters is what the fund owns, how it is constructed, and how it behaves in stressed markets. A broad U.S. equity ETF and a narrowly focused semiconductor ETF may both trade on an exchange and both be called ETFs, but their risk profiles can be radically different. The label does not guarantee balance, stability, or protection from loss. Investors sometimes confuse the convenience of the structure with safety, when the real source of risk still comes from the underlying holdings.

A related misunderstanding is that all ETFs are passive and therefore identical in behavior. Many ETFs do track indexes, but the index itself may be broad, concentrated, rules-based, or unusually complex. Others are actively managed and may trade more frequently or hold more concentrated positions. Even among index ETFs, the methodology can create meaningful differences in sector weights, rebalancing timing, turnover, and tax behavior. The practical point is that "ETF" does not tell you enough by itself. Two funds can use the same asset class label and still produce different results because the selection rules are not the same.

Another limitation investors should understand is that ETFs can be more liquid in appearance than in economic reality. The ability to buy and sell shares throughout the day is valuable, but that does not mean every ETF is equally easy to trade well. Some funds have tight bid-ask spreads and deep underlying markets; others may trade infrequently, with wider spreads or larger price swings around the quoted market price. This distinction matters most when investors use market orders, trade during volatile periods, or move in and out of less liquid strategies. The exchange listing makes trading possible, but it does not eliminate execution risk.

It is also a mistake to assume that ETFs always reduce taxes. Many broad index ETFs are tax-efficient because of how they manage portfolio turnover and in-kind transactions, but tax outcomes vary by fund type, asset class, and account type. Bond ETFs, commodity ETFs, and certain actively managed or niche strategies may generate taxable distributions or other tax complications that are less favorable than investors expect. Tax efficiency is a benefit of some ETFs, not a universal feature of all ETFs. The same is true for cost: a low expense ratio is important, but it does not capture the full cost of ownership if trading spreads, premiums, discounts, or turnover are meaningful.

Investors also sometimes overstate the precision of ETF exposure. An ETF may be described as tracking a market, sector, or factor, yet its actual holdings can differ from the broad label in ways that matter. Index construction rules, sampling methods, and rebalancing schedules all influence the final portfolio. That means an investor seeking a very specific exposure should not rely on the fund name alone. Looking through to the holdings and methodology is essential, especially when the strategy is thematic or factor-based. Research on trading strategies and market behavior also shows that performance can vary substantially depending on how a portfolio is selected and maintained [30]. In other words, the rules behind the fund are part of the investment result.

There is also a behavioral misconception worth correcting: because ETFs are easy to trade, they are often treated as if they are meant to be traded frequently. Ease of access can invite overconfidence, short-term reactions, and unnecessary turnover. The ability to act quickly is not the same as having a reason to act quickly. Investors may also assume that a popular ETF has been "validated" by the market, when popularity can simply reflect recent performance, marketing visibility, or a narrow investor theme. As financial products multiply and become more specialized, the burden on the investor increases rather than decreases. Regulatory discussions around investor protection have long emphasized that product access does not remove the need for informed use [33].

Finally, ETFs have real limitations in portfolio construction. They are efficient tools, but they do not solve every investing problem. They cannot eliminate market risk, and they cannot compensate for a poorly chosen asset allocation. A portfolio built entirely from highly correlated ETFs can still be fragile, even if it appears diversified by ticker count. Some strategies may also be difficult to evaluate because their underlying indexes or holdings change in ways that are not immediately obvious. For investors interested in responsible, thematic, or specialized exposures, the challenge is often not finding an ETF but finding one whose structure, holdings, and objectives actually match the intended role in the portfolio [32]. The most useful way to think about ETFs is not as a guarantee of good investing, but as a flexible instrument that still requires judgment, discipline, and due diligence.

CHAPTER 2

Chapter 2: The ETF Landscape and Core Categories

The ETF market is best understood as a menu of exposures rather than a single product category, and the differences among those exposures matter as much as the exchange-traded wrapper itself. Some ETFs are designed to capture broad market segments, while others narrow the focus to a sector, a region, a factor, or a specific investment objective. That range gives investors flexibility, but it also means that two funds with similar trading features can behave very differently once market conditions change. The category label can suggest a starting point, yet it does not reveal everything about concentration, sensitivity to economic cycles, or the role a fund may play in a portfolio.

Broad market, sector, and style ETFs

Broad market ETFs are the most straightforward way to buy a large slice of a stock or bond market in a single transaction. In equities, these funds are usually built around well-known benchmarks such as the S&P 500, the total U.S. market, or developed international indexes. Their purpose is not to make a sharp bet on one industry, one company, or one economic outcome, but to provide diversified exposure that can serve as a portfolio core. Because the holdings are spread across many securities, the fund's return is driven primarily by the performance of the market segment it tracks, not by any one position. That makes broad market

ETFs useful for investors who want to keep implementation simple while still participating in the long-term growth of stocks or the income and stability characteristics of bonds.

The practical appeal of broad market ETFs is that they reduce the need to forecast which part of the market will lead next. A single fund can provide exposure to hundreds or even thousands of companies, which helps limit the impact of any one firm's earnings miss, management change, or regulatory problem. This does not eliminate market risk, but it does make the portfolio less dependent on isolated events. For many investors, broad market ETFs are the default building block because they create a foundation that can later be complemented with more targeted exposures. Their role is often less about excitement and more about consistency, discipline, and efficient access to a diversified return stream.

Sector ETFs, by contrast, isolate a specific part of the economy such as technology, financials, health care, energy, or utilities. They are useful when an investor wants to emphasize a particular industry group, express a view on business conditions, or adjust the portfolio's sensitivity to economic cycles. A sector fund can outperform the broad market when its industry is in favor, but it can also lag badly when conditions turn against it. That concentration is the defining feature of the category. A sector ETF is therefore not a substitute for diversification; it is a deliberate narrowing of exposure. Investors should understand that sector funds often contain many companies, yet they remain concentrated because those companies are linked by the same economic drivers, regulatory pressures, and competitive forces.

Sector ETFs can also behave very differently from one another even when they sound similar. Some sectors are heavily influenced by interest rates, some by commodity prices, some by consumer spending, and some by technological change. For example, a fund focused on banks may respond to yield-curve shifts and credit conditions, while a fund focused on energy may be affected more by oil prices and capital expenditure trends. This is why sector ETFs are often used tactically rather than as permanent core holdings. They can be valuable tools for investors who understand the underlying business cycle exposure, but they require more attention than broad market funds because their fortunes are tied to narrower conditions.

Style ETFs add another layer of selection by organizing stocks according to characteristics such as market capitalization, valuation, growth orientation, profitability, or volatility. The most familiar style distinctions are large-cap, mid-cap, and small-cap, along with growth and value. A large-cap ETF tends to emphasize bigger, more established companies, while a small-cap ETF reaches further down the market-cap spectrum and may carry greater sensitivity to economic expansion, financing conditions, and company-specific uncertainty. Growth and value funds, meanwhile, tilt toward different types of business profiles and market expectations. Growth-oriented funds often hold companies priced for faster earnings expansion, while value-oriented funds generally emphasize stocks that appear cheaper relative to fundamentals.

Style categories are useful because they help investors shape the character of their equity exposure without having to pick individual stocks. They can also be combined to express a more precise portfolio stance. An investor may want broad market exposure but with a tilt toward smaller companies, or a core allocation to large-cap stocks with a modest value bias. At the same time, style ETFs can become a source of hidden concentration if used without discipline. A portfolio that appears diversified across multiple funds may in fact lean heavily toward one style factor, one market segment, or one region. The label on the fund is only the starting point; the actual holdings and index rules determine how much diversification the investor really has.

Understanding the differences among broad market, sector, and style ETFs matters because each category serves a different role in portfolio construction. Broad market funds are generally the most efficient way to establish a core allocation. Sector ETFs are more concentrated and are best understood as targeted tilts or tactical tools. Style ETFs sit between those two poles, offering a way to refine the market exposure already in place. The same investor may use all three, but not for the same purpose. A retirement account built for long-term accumulation may rely primarily on broad market ETFs, while sector and style funds may be used sparingly to adjust risk, express a view, or complement an existing core.

The distinction becomes even more important when investors evaluate what they already own. Two ETFs can both be labeled "equity" funds and still produce very different portfolio effects. One may track the entire market, another may concentrate in a single industry, and a third may overweight a style segment that already dominates the investor's holdings. Because of that, the real question is not whether an ETF is broad, sector-specific, or style-oriented in name, but how it changes the overall balance of the portfolio. In practice, that means looking past the label and asking what part of the market the fund actually owns, how concentrated it is, and whether it adds something distinct or simply repeats exposure already present elsewhere.

Bond, commodity, and cash-equivalent ETFs

Bond ETFs are often used for one of two reasons: to build a more stable core in a portfolio, or to fine-tune a specific interest rate and credit exposure. Unlike stock ETFs, which are usually discussed in terms of growth and valuation, bond ETFs are shaped by maturity, duration, credit quality, and the structure of the underlying bond market. Those features matter because bond prices respond differently to changes in rates, inflation expectations, and issuer credit conditions. A long-duration Treasury ETF, for example, will react much more sharply to interest rate changes than a short-term government bond ETF, even though both are "bond funds." Investors who treat all bond ETFs as interchangeable can misunderstand both their defensive role and their risk profile.

Within fixed income, the most important distinctions are usually issuer type and duration. Government bond ETFs may hold Treasury securities or other sovereign issues, and they are often used for capital preservation or liquidity management. Investment-grade corporate bond ETFs add credit exposure in exchange for higher yields, but that extra income comes with greater sensitivity to economic stress and spread widening. High-yield bond ETFs can offer even more income, yet they behave less like traditional ballast and more like a hybrid between credit and equity risk during market drawdowns. Duration adds another layer: shorter-duration funds tend to be less volatile, while intermediate- and long-duration funds are more exposed to changes in market interest rates. In practice, the "bond" label tells you very little unless you also know what kind of bonds the fund owns and how long those bonds take to mature.

Bond ETFs are also useful because they make a fragmented market easier to access. Individual bonds can be difficult to trade efficiently, especially in less liquid segments of the market, and pricing can vary across dealers and transaction sizes. A bond ETF pools many securities into a single instrument that can be bought and sold during the trading day, which simplifies implementation for investors who want broad exposure without managing dozens of separate positions. That convenience has helped bond ETFs become an important part of portfolio construction, particularly for investors seeking efficient access to corporate and government debt markets. At the same time, the ETF wrapper does not eliminate the underlying risks of the bonds it holds. It mainly changes how those risks are packaged and traded.

Commodity ETFs serve a different purpose. They are often used as a diversifier, an inflation-sensitive allocation, or a way to gain exposure to assets that do not move in lockstep with stocks and bonds. Research has long examined commodities as an investment because they can provide diversification benefits that are distinct from traditional financial assets [9][49]. Commodity ETFs may track a broad commodity index, a single commodity such as gold or oil, or a basket of futures contracts. The structure matters here as well. Many commodity ETFs do not hold the physical commodity itself; instead, they gain exposure through futures, swaps, or other derivatives. That means performance can be influenced not only by the spot price of the commodity, but also by futures curve effects such as contango and backwardation, rollover costs, and collateral returns. An investor who expects a commodity ETF to move exactly with the cash price of oil or wheat may be disappointed if the futures structure is unfavorable.

Because commodity exposure is often obtained through derivatives, these funds can behave differently from the underlying commodity that headlines describe. Gold ETFs are a common exception in the sense that some are backed by physical bullion, which can make their behavior more straightforward than that of many broad commodity funds. Even then, the investor still needs to understand storage, insurance, and tracking considerations. Broad commodity ETFs, by contrast, are usually better understood as portfolio tools than as direct substitutes for owning raw materials. They are typically used in moderation, because commodities can be volatile and may produce long periods of weak returns even when they serve a useful diversification role. Their value is often less about steady appreciation and more about how they respond when inflation, supply shocks, or geopolitical stress affect other asset classes.

Cash-equivalent ETFs occupy the most conservative end of the spectrum. These funds are designed to provide highly liquid exposure to short-term, low-duration instruments such as Treasury bills, government money market instruments, or very short-term bond portfolios. They are often used for temporary cash management, rebalancing reserves, or holding funds that may soon be deployed elsewhere. Their appeal lies in simplicity and liquidity: they are easier to trade than many individual short-term instruments, and they can be held in brokerage accounts with the same convenience as other ETFs. But “cash-equivalent” should not be confused with “cash.” These ETFs can fluctuate in price, however modestly, and they can decline when short-term rates move or when the fund’s holdings reprice.

The role of cash-equivalent ETFs is therefore operational as much as investment-driven. They can serve as a parking place for assets awaiting a new allocation, a buffer for withdrawals, or a way to earn a modest yield while preserving a high degree of accessibility. During periods when investors want to reduce risk without leaving the market ecosystem entirely, these funds can be a practical tool. Still, they are not a guarantee against loss, and they are not identical to insured bank deposits. Their yields and prices depend on the short end of the interest rate market, fund expenses, and the specific instruments held inside the portfolio. As with other ETF categories, the label describes the general purpose, but the actual holdings and structure determine how the fund behaves when conditions change.

International and emerging market ETFs

International and emerging market ETFs give investors access to companies, governments, and currencies outside their home market, but the category is broader than a simple “foreign stocks” label suggests. A developed-market international ETF may focus on large, liquid businesses in Europe, Japan, Canada, or Australia, while an emerging market ETF may hold firms in economies with faster growth potential, less mature market structures, and greater sensitivity to political and currency shifts. The distinction matters because the return experience of these funds is shaped not only by corporate earnings, but also by exchange rates, local inflation, policy decisions, and the degree to which markets are integrated with global capital flows. International allocation is therefore not just a question of geography; it is a question of how an investor wants to diversify economic exposure.

For many U.S.-based investors, international ETFs are used to reduce reliance on a single country’s economic cycle and valuation regime. That role has become more important as global portfolios increasingly respond to benchmark-driven allocation patterns, with large pools of capital moving in ways that reinforce certain market weights [25]. A broad international ETF can help offset the concentration that often develops when a portfolio is built primarily around domestic equities. It may also provide exposure to industries and business models that are underrepresented at home, such as global luxury brands, industrial exporters, or multinational financial firms. Emerging market ETFs can add a different layer of diversification, since their earnings drivers may be tied more closely to domestic consumption, infrastructure growth, or commodity demand than to the same factors that dominate developed markets.

At the same time, the diversification benefit should not be confused with smooth performance. International and emerging market ETFs often carry currency risk, which can either help or hurt returns depending on the relative movement of the investor’s home currency and the local currency of the holdings. They can also be affected by political risk, capital controls, weaker shareholder protections, lower disclosure quality, and uneven market liquidity. These issues are especially relevant in emerging markets, where the institutional environment may be less stable and where a single policy change can affect entire sectors. Investors sometimes focus on headline growth rates and overlook the fact that faster economic expansion does not automatically translate into stronger stock returns.

Index construction is especially important in this category. Some ETFs track market-cap-weighted indexes, which means a small number of large countries or companies can dominate the portfolio. Others use country caps, regional screens, or factor-based rules that change the balance of exposure. An ETF labeled "emerging markets" may therefore look very different from another fund with the same broad description. One fund may be heavily tilted toward financials and technology in Asia, while another may have more exposure to energy, materials, or state-influenced enterprises. Investors who want a more precise allocation need to look beyond the country label and examine the actual holdings, sector weights, and benchmark methodology.

Costs and trading behavior also deserve attention. International ETFs can have wider bid-ask spreads than large domestic funds, especially when the underlying markets are closed or when the ETF holds securities that are harder to price in real time. That means the market price of the ETF may move differently from the last quoted value of its holdings during the U.S. trading day. Emerging market funds can show this effect more clearly because local exchanges may operate on different schedules, and some underlying securities may be less liquid. For investors placing larger trades, the apparent simplicity of a ticker symbol can hide meaningful implementation costs if the fund is thinly traded or if the underlying market is fragmented.

Tax treatment is another practical consideration. International ETFs may hold foreign securities that generate withholding taxes on dividends, and the treatment can vary by fund structure and account type. In addition, some international funds are designed to provide geographic exposure, while others are built to deliver a specific income profile, sector tilt, or sustainability screen. That distinction matters because the fund's objective can influence both its risk profile and its turnover. ESG-themed international funds, for example, may use index rules that exclude certain industries or weight companies differently from the broader market. Research on ESG and themed funds suggests that label and implementation are not the same thing; what a fund claims to emphasize does not always translate cleanly into the characteristics of the portfolio it actually holds [24][26][21].

Investors also need to think about how international exposure interacts with the rest of the portfolio. A domestic-heavy portfolio can benefit from a measured allocation to developed and emerging markets, but the appropriate split depends on existing holdings, time horizon, and tolerance for volatility. Some investors prefer a core international developed-market ETF with a smaller satellite position in emerging markets, while others combine both in a single all-world fund for simplicity. Either approach can be reasonable. The key is to avoid assuming that "international" automatically means "balanced." A fund concentrated in a few large countries, or one dominated by a narrow set of sectors, may still leave the portfolio exposed to the same kinds of concentration risk that investors were trying to reduce in the first place.

Thematic, smart beta, and actively managed ETFs

Thematic ETFs are built around a specific idea, trend, or long-term narrative rather than a broad market segment. They may focus on clean energy, artificial intelligence, cybersecurity, robotics, aging populations, or another theme that the sponsor believes could reshape the economy over time. This structure can be appealing because it gives investors a way to express a view without having to identify individual winners. The tradeoff is that themes are usually narrower than traditional sector funds and often more concentrated than broad index ETFs. A theme can be compelling intellectually and still produce uneven results if the underlying companies are expensive, early in their business cycle, or highly sensitive to changing investor sentiment.

Because thematic funds are built around a story, they often attract capital at the same time the story is already popular. That timing matters. When a theme becomes widely discussed, the ETF may gather assets after much of the initial rerating has already occurred. In other words, the fund can be buying into momentum rather than discovering overlooked value. Thematic ETFs also tend to vary in how strictly they define the theme. One provider may use revenue thresholds tied to a specific business activity, while another may include companies with only partial exposure. As a result, two funds with similar names can hold very different portfolios and deliver very different outcomes. Investors need to look past the label and examine the actual holdings, inclusion rules, and rebalancing process.

Smart beta ETFs sit between traditional passive indexing and discretionary active management. Instead of weighting companies purely by market capitalization, they use rules to tilt the portfolio toward characteristics such as value, quality, momentum, low volatility, dividend yield, or size. The idea is not simply to own the market as it is, but to capture a persistent factor or structural bias in a systematic way. This can be useful for investors who want a more deliberate exposure than a plain market-cap index offers, without relying on a manager to make security-by-security judgments. In that sense, smart beta is often best understood as rules-based active exposure packaged in an index-like form [42].

The appeal of smart beta is that it can address perceived shortcomings of market-cap weighting. A cap-weighted index naturally gives more weight to the largest companies, even when those companies are expensive or concentrated in a few industries. A smart beta strategy may reduce that concentration or emphasize attributes associated with stronger long-term outcomes. But factor investing is not a free lunch. Factors can go through long periods of underperformance, and the very characteristics that help in one market environment can lag in another. A low-volatility ETF may hold up better in turbulent markets but trail sharply in strong risk-on rallies. A value ETF may look attractive after a long slump, yet still require patience before the valuation advantage is reflected in returns. The investor must be prepared to own the factor through cycles, not just when it is recently in favor.

Actively managed ETFs use a portfolio manager or management team to select securities, adjust weights, and respond to market conditions within the ETF structure. They may seek to outperform a benchmark, generate income, manage downside risk, or pursue a specialized strategy that is difficult to capture with a simple rules-based index. Compared with a traditional mutual fund, an active ETF offers the exchange-traded wrapper, which can improve trading flexibility and, in some cases, tax efficiency. But the presence of an ETF wrapper does not eliminate the core question of active management: whether the manager has a durable edge after fees, trading costs, and the possibility of style drift are considered. The wrapper changes the delivery mechanism, not the underlying challenge of consistent outperformance.

For investors evaluating these categories, the most important question is not whether the fund is labeled thematic, smart beta, or active, but what problem it is meant to solve in the portfolio. A thematic ETF may be appropriate as a small satellite position when an investor wants targeted exposure to a long-duration trend. A smart beta ETF may be useful when the goal is to tilt toward a factor that complements the rest of the portfolio. An active ETF may make sense when the strategy depends on judgment, security selection, or a less efficient segment of the market. In each case, the position size should reflect uncertainty. Narrower ideas deserve smaller allocations because the range of outcomes is wider.

These products also require closer scrutiny of methodology than many broad-market ETFs. For thematic and smart beta funds, the index rules determine which companies qualify, how much each holding receives, and how often the portfolio is rebalanced. For active ETFs, the manager's process, turnover, and benchmark awareness matter just as much. Investors should pay attention to concentration, overlap with existing holdings, and whether the fund is truly adding a distinct exposure or simply repackaging familiar stocks under a new label. This is especially important in ESG-oriented or sustainability-themed ETFs, where research has shown that definitions, metrics, and methodologies can vary widely across providers [54]. The same general caution applies to any strategy built around a narrative: the more specific the story, the more important it is to verify the actual portfolio mechanics behind it.

CHAPTER 3

Chapter 3: How ETFs Are Built and Traded

To understand an ETF properly, it helps to look beneath the ticker symbol and see the machinery that makes the fund trade the way it does. An ETF is not simply a list of holdings packaged for convenience; it is a structure built around creation, redemption, pricing, and market access, all of which shape how investors experience the fund in real time. Those mechanics are often invisible when markets are calm, yet they become especially important when trading volume rises, sentiment shifts quickly, or the underlying securities are less liquid than the ETF itself appears to be.

ETF structure: baskets, shares, and net asset value

An ETF is built from a basket of securities, but that basket is not the whole story. The fund sponsor decides which assets belong in the basket, how they are weighted, how often they are rebalanced, and how closely the portfolio is meant to mirror an index or strategy. That basket may contain hundreds of stocks, a smaller set of bonds, commodities through linked instruments, or a mix of exposures designed to track a particular segment of the market. In practical terms, the basket is the portfolio engine inside the ETF wrapper. It is what gives the fund its economic exposure, while the exchange-traded shares are simply the way investors access that exposure.

Those shares are issued in the same way for every ETF investor: they represent a fractional claim on the fund's assets, not direct ownership of each underlying security. When you buy one share of an ETF, you are buying a small slice of the fund's total pool, and the value of that slice rises or falls with the value of the underlying holdings. This is why two ETFs with similar share prices can still differ greatly in what they actually own and how they behave. The share price itself is not the same thing as the value of the portfolio. A fund can split shares, launch with a low initial price, or trade at a level that is more convenient for market participants, but none of that changes the economic substance of the holdings.

Net asset value, or NAV, is the accounting measure that ties the whole structure together. It is calculated by taking the market value of the fund's assets, subtracting liabilities, and dividing the result by the number of shares outstanding. In other words, NAV is the per-share value of the portfolio after expenses and obligations are accounted for. For funds holding highly liquid securities, NAV is usually very close to the price at which the ETF trades during the day, but the two are not identical concepts. NAV is a valuation measure, while the market price is the price buyers and sellers agree on in the exchange. The relationship between them is one of the most important features of ETF trading because it is what helps keep prices aligned with the value of the underlying basket.

This alignment is maintained through the creation and redemption process. When demand for ETF shares increases, authorized participants can create new shares by delivering the appropriate basket of securities to the fund, or cash in some structures, in exchange for newly issued ETF shares. When demand weakens, they can redeem shares and receive the underlying basket back. That mechanism gives the ETF a built-in supply channel that helps prevent persistent gaps between market price and NAV. It also explains why ETFs can often absorb large inflows or outflows without the kind of forced buying and selling that would otherwise be required in a closed pool of assets. Research on ETF structure has also shown that replication method matters: physically backed and synthetic approaches can carry different sources of tracking error and risk [61].

For investors, the important point is that the basket, the shares, and the NAV each play a different role. The basket determines what exposure the fund actually delivers. The shares determine how that exposure is packaged for trading. The NAV provides the reference point for whether the market price is fair relative to the portfolio's value. When these elements work together smoothly, the ETF can trade efficiently and remain close to its underlying value. When they do not, the differences tend to show up as premiums, discounts, wider spreads, or tracking differences that are especially noticeable in less liquid markets or during periods of stress.

The composition of the basket also affects how the ETF functions in the market. A fund holding highly liquid large-cap stocks can usually be created and redeemed more easily than a fund holding thinly traded bonds, frontier-market securities, or other instruments that are harder to source and price. That difference matters because the ease of assembling the basket influences how efficiently the creation-redemption process works. In less liquid markets, the fund may rely more heavily on pricing estimates, dealer quotes, or other valuation inputs, which can make NAV less exact in real time. This is one reason bond ETFs and other fixed-income products can sometimes show more visible differences between market price and estimated portfolio value than broad equity ETFs.

It is also useful to remember that not all baskets are assembled in the same way. Some ETFs hold the underlying securities directly, while others use derivatives or swap arrangements to replicate returns. Both structures can serve the same investment objective, but they do not do so through identical risk channels. A physical fund depends on the securities it owns outright, while a synthetic fund adds counterparty and contract-related considerations on top of market exposure [61]. For an investor, the distinction is not merely technical. It affects how the fund sources returns, how it may behave when markets are dislocated, and how closely it may track its stated benchmark over time.

The result is that an ETF should be understood as a system rather than a single object. The basket defines the portfolio, the shares define the tradable unit, and NAV defines the fund's underlying value. Once those pieces are clear, the later questions in ETF analysis become easier to handle: how price stays aligned with value, why spreads widen or narrow, and why some funds trade almost like their holdings while others can behave in more complicated ways. The structure is what gives ETFs their flexibility, but it is also what determines the limits of that flexibility.

Primary market versus secondary market trading

ETF trading takes place in two related but distinct arenas. The secondary market is the one most investors see directly: it is the exchange where ETF shares change hands between buyers and sellers during the trading day. The primary market is less visible. It is where authorized participants, typically large institutions, create new ETF shares or redeem existing ones by exchanging the underlying basket of securities, or a cash equivalent, with the fund sponsor. The two markets work together, but they serve different functions. The secondary market provides access and price discovery for everyday investors, while the primary market helps keep the ETF aligned with the value of its holdings.

In the secondary market, an investor simply places an order through a brokerage account, and the trade is executed against another market participant. The ETF's share price is set continuously by supply and demand, just as with a stock. That means the quoted market price can move above or below the fund's underlying value during the day, especially when markets are volatile or when the ETF holds less liquid securities. For most investors, this is the only market they need to think about when buying or selling shares. The experience is straightforward: the investor sees a bid, an ask, and a tradeable market price.

The primary market, by contrast, is the mechanism that allows the ETF share count to expand or contract. If demand for an ETF rises and the shares begin to trade at a premium to the value of the underlying basket, an authorized participant can buy the underlying securities, deliver them to the fund, and receive newly created ETF shares. Those shares can then be sold into the secondary market, increasing supply and helping push the ETF price back toward its underlying value. The reverse process works when shares trade at a discount: an authorized participant can buy ETF shares in the market, redeem them with the fund, and receive the underlying basket, reducing supply and helping narrow the discount. This creation and redemption process is one reason ETFs can remain closely linked to the value of their holdings even though they trade intraday.

That linkage is important because it explains why ETF pricing is not merely a matter of one market "following" another. The secondary market sets the price investors see, but the primary market provides the arbitrage pressure that discourages persistent mispricing. In efficient conditions, when the ETF's market price begins to drift away from net asset value, the creation and redemption process creates an economic incentive for large market participants to step in. The result is a self-correcting structure that supports liquidity and price alignment. This is one reason the ETF wrapper has become so useful in modern passive investing, where low-cost exposure and tradability are both central goals [53].

Still, the relationship is not perfectly frictionless. The primary market depends on the ability of authorized participants to assemble or dispose of the underlying basket at a reasonable cost. If the ETF holds securities that are difficult to trade, if the market is under stress, or if the underlying assets themselves are not priced continuously, then creation and redemption can become more expensive or less attractive. In those cases, the ETF may still trade efficiently, but the gap between the exchange price and the fund's underlying value can widen temporarily. This is especially relevant for funds holding less liquid bonds, niche international securities, or specialized strategies where valuation and execution are less straightforward.

Investors should also understand that the primary market does not mean retail investors can walk directly into the fund and exchange shares for the underlying basket. That privilege is reserved for authorized participants and, in practice, for a small set of large institutions with the operational capacity to handle baskets, settlement, and market-making activity. For the individual investor, the practical implication is simpler: when you buy or sell an ETF, you are almost always interacting with the secondary market, while the primary market sits behind the scenes maintaining the structure. This division of labor is a key part of why ETFs can combine stock-like trading with fund-like diversification.

The distinction matters most when an investor evaluates execution quality. A highly liquid ETF may have active trading on the exchange even if the underlying market is only moderately liquid, because the primary market can still help absorb imbalances. But a narrow bid-ask spread in the ETF itself does not guarantee that every trade will be efficient in all conditions, just as a large fund size does not eliminate the possibility of temporary premiums or discounts. The best way to think about ETF trading is that the secondary market is where your order is filled, while the primary market is the mechanism that helps keep that fill close to the value of the portfolio underneath it. Understanding both layers makes it easier to judge when a quoted price is normal market noise and when it may reflect a more meaningful dislocation.

Bid-ask spreads, premiums, and discounts

For an ETF investor, the quoted share price is only part of the trading cost. The difference between the best price a buyer is willing to pay and the best price a seller is willing to accept is the bid-ask spread, and that spread is often the first friction an investor encounters when entering or exiting a position. In a highly liquid ETF, the spread may be only a penny or two for a large, widely traded fund. In a thinner market, or in a fund holding less liquid assets, the spread can widen enough to matter, especially for frequent traders or for larger orders. The spread is not a fee charged by the fund sponsor, but it is a real cost embedded in execution. A buyer who pays the ask and later sells at the bid has effectively paid the spread, even if the fund's published expense ratio looks low.

The spread reflects the market's short-term view of supply, demand, and the difficulty of hedging the underlying portfolio. When trading is active and the ETF's holdings are easy to price, market makers can quote tighter prices because they can manage inventory and risk efficiently. When conditions are uncertain, spreads often widen. This is especially noticeable in market segments where the underlying securities trade less frequently, such as some high-yield bonds, emerging market debt, or niche equity themes. Passive investing has expanded dramatically because of its low cost and diversification benefits [53], but low fund expenses do not eliminate the trading friction that can arise at the point of execution.

Premiums and discounts are related but distinct from the bid-ask spread. An ETF trades at a premium when its market price is above the value of its underlying holdings, and at a discount when its market price is below that value. The reference point is the fund's net asset value, or NAV, which is calculated from the market value of the portfolio holdings. In a well-functioning ETF, premiums and discounts are usually small and temporary because the creation and redemption process gives authorized participants an incentive to arbitrage price gaps. If the ETF trades too far above NAV, arbitrageurs can create shares and sell them; if it trades too far below NAV, they can buy shares and redeem them. That mechanism helps keep market price and NAV aligned, though it does not eliminate short-term deviations.

It is important not to confuse a premium or discount with good or bad fund quality by itself. A small, brief discount does not necessarily mean the ETF is broken, just as a small premium does not mean the fund is expensive in a fundamental sense. The more useful question is whether price deviations are persistent, unusually large, or occurring in a product whose underlying assets are hard to trade. Funds holding instruments that are less transparent or less liquid can show wider gaps between market price and NAV during stressed periods, because the market may be uncertain about the true value of the portfolio. Research on market stress has shown that ETF behavior can vary meaningfully across fund types, with results depending on the liquidity and risk characteristics of the underlying holdings [46].

For investors, the practical issue is how these pricing features affect execution. A market order entered during a calm, liquid session may fill near the midpoint of the spread and close to NAV, creating little visible friction. The same order entered when spreads are wide or when the market is moving quickly can produce a noticeably worse fill. That is why the quoted spread, the time of day, and the liquidity of the underlying market all matter. A broad equity ETF traded during normal market hours will usually be easier to execute efficiently than a specialized bond or thematic fund. The fact that an ETF trades on an exchange does not guarantee that every share changes hands at a fair price at every moment; it means the price discovery process is continuous rather than once per day.

Investors can also misread a discount as a bargain. If an ETF is trading below NAV, the instinct may be to see an immediate opportunity. Sometimes that is reasonable, but only if the discount is temporary and not explained by trading conditions, stale pricing in the underlying market, or a structural feature of the fund. The same caution applies to premiums: a fund that is trading above NAV may still be a sensible purchase if the premium is small and the investor has a long horizon, but repeated purchases at inflated prices add avoidable drag. This is one reason ETF due diligence should include not only the fund's strategy and expense ratio, but also its typical spread behavior and the quality of its secondary-market trading.

In practice, investors reduce these costs by using limit orders when conditions are uncertain, avoiding the open and close when spreads may be less stable, and paying attention to the liquidity of the underlying market rather than the ETF ticker alone. The best-known ETF is not automatically the cheapest to trade if the market is moving rapidly or if the order size is unusually large. Bid-ask spreads, premiums, and discounts are part of the real economics of ETF investing, and understanding them helps investors distinguish between the fund's stated cost and the price actually paid in the market.

Trading mechanics, order types, and execution basics

Once an ETF is in your portfolio, the mechanics of how you enter and exit the position matter more than many investors first assume. The same fund can produce very different outcomes depending on whether the order is placed during a calm trading period, near the open or close of the market, or in a thinly traded session. Because ETF shares trade on an exchange, the execution price is not set by the fund company in the way a mutual fund's end-of-day transaction is. It is negotiated continuously in the market, and that means the investor's order behavior becomes part of the result.

The most basic choice is between a market order and a limit order. A market order instructs your broker to buy or sell immediately at the best available price. That approach prioritizes speed, which can be useful for highly liquid, broad-market ETFs when the spread is tight and trading volume is deep. The tradeoff is that the final execution price may differ from the last quoted price, especially if the market is moving quickly or the order book is thin. A limit order, by contrast, sets the maximum price you are willing to pay when buying or the minimum price you are willing to accept when selling. This gives you price control, but it does not guarantee execution. In practice, limit orders are often the more deliberate choice for ETFs with wider spreads, lower volume, or more volatile underlying markets.

Stop orders and stop-limit orders add another layer of control, but they also introduce additional complexity. A stop order becomes a market order once a specified trigger price is reached, which can help investors automate an exit if a position moves against them. The drawback is that the fill can occur at a price materially worse than the trigger in a fast market. A stop-limit order attempts to reduce that risk by converting into a limit order after the trigger is reached, but then the same limitation applies: if the market moves through the limit price too quickly, the order may not execute at all. These orders are not inherently better or worse than market or limit orders; they simply serve different purposes, and they are most useful when the investor has a clear reason for defining an exit condition in advance.

Execution quality depends not only on the order type, but also on the timing and size of the trade. ETFs often trade with the greatest depth after the market has opened and before the close, when liquidity providers are more active and price discovery is more efficient. The first and last minutes of the session can be especially noisy because prices are adjusting to overnight information or end-of-day imbalances. For that reason, large orders are often better handled with patience rather than urgency. Splitting a trade into smaller pieces, using limit prices, or working the order through the day can reduce the chance of paying an unnecessary premium. This is particularly relevant for funds holding less liquid securities, where the ETF's market price may react more sharply to short-term supply and demand.

It is also important to distinguish between the ETF's share price and the value of the portfolio it represents. The market price may trade slightly above or below the fund's underlying value, and those differences can shift intraday as buyers and sellers interact. In a well-functioning ETF, arbitrage activity by authorized participants helps keep the share price close to the value of the holdings, but that process is not instantaneous and does not eliminate short-term execution risk. Investors who place aggressive market orders during periods of stress may experience slippage, which is the gap between the expected price and the actual fill. Slippage is not unique to ETFs, but because ETFs are traded instruments, it can become a meaningful part of the total cost of a transaction.

Order routing and trading venue can matter as well. Many investors assume that all exchange-listed securities are effectively the same once they are in the market, but liquidity can be fragmented across venues, and displayed quotes are not always the whole picture. For most investors, the practical implication is simple: use a broker with reliable execution tools, check whether the ETF is actively traded, and avoid assuming that the last quoted price is the price you will receive. In especially liquid funds, the difference may be trivial. In more specialized ETFs, the spread, the time of day, and the urgency of the order can all influence the final cost more than the stated expense ratio for that day's trade.

For investors using ETFs in a portfolio context, execution should match intent. A long-term allocation trade often does not require speed, so a limit order placed during normal market hours may be more appropriate than a market order sent impulsively at the open. A tactical trade, where the goal is to establish exposure quickly after a decision has already been made, may justify a more aggressive approach if the ETF is highly liquid. In either case, the discipline lies in recognizing that trading an ETF is not just a matter of selecting a fund; it is also a matter of choosing how to interact with the market that prices the fund. The better that choice matches the fund's liquidity and the investor's time horizon, the more efficiently the position is likely to be established.

CHAPTER 4

Chapter 4: Evaluating ETF Quality Before You Buy

Before an ETF earns a place in a portfolio, it should be judged as a product, not just a ticker. Two funds can pursue the same market exposure and still leave an investor with very different outcomes once fees, execution, index design, and sponsor practices are taken into account. That is why the apparent simplicity of an ETF should not replace a careful review of what the fund actually costs to hold, how faithfully it behaves relative to its stated benchmark, and how well its structure supports efficient trading. The quality of the wrapper matters because it influences not only return potential, but also the reliability and consistency of the exposure being purchased.

Expense ratios, trading costs, and total ownership cost

The expense ratio is the easiest cost to see, but it is only one part of what an investor pays to own an ETF. It is the annual fee charged by the fund and deducted from assets inside the portfolio, so it reduces returns automatically rather than arriving as a separate bill. Because it is expressed as a percentage, it can look small in isolation, especially when compared with the size of a portfolio or the volatility of the markets. Yet over time it matters because it is paid every year, regardless of whether the fund rises or falls. A difference of a few basis points may seem minor in one calendar year, but over a long holding period it can meaningfully affect compound growth.

That said, the lowest expense ratio is not always the best choice. A fund's cost has to be judged alongside what it delivers: the market exposure, the quality of the index or strategy, the efficiency of the portfolio management, and the likelihood that the fund will actually behave as expected. Some ETFs charge more because they operate in less efficient markets, use more complex implementation methods, or require more active oversight. In those cases, the fee may still be reasonable if the fund provides access or precision that a cheaper alternative cannot. Cost matters, but it should be interpreted in context rather than treated as a stand-alone ranking system.

Trading costs are the second layer of ownership cost, and they are often more variable than the expense ratio. The most visible trading cost is the bid-ask spread, which is the gap between the price a buyer pays and the price a seller receives. Investors who trade frequently, place market orders in thinly traded funds, or buy and sell during volatile periods may pay more through spreads than they realize. Commission costs are lower than they once were at many brokers, but they have not disappeared entirely, and institutional-style execution issues can still arise through poor order placement, unfavorable timing, or crossing a wide spread. An ETF with a tiny expense ratio can still be expensive to trade if its shares are illiquid or its underlying holdings are difficult to price quickly.

The relationship between trading cost and fund size is important but not always linear. A heavily traded ETF with a deep market in its shares may be inexpensive to enter and exit even if the underlying securities are not especially liquid, because market makers can often manage the creation and redemption process efficiently. By contrast, a less popular fund may have a narrow strategy, a thin secondary market, or a wider spread that raises the cost of each transaction. This is one reason investors should distinguish between the fund's stated operating cost and the cost of implementing a position in real time. The first is recurring and predictable the second depends on how and when the trade is made.

Total ownership cost combines these visible and invisible expenses into a more realistic picture. For a long-term investor, that includes the expense ratio, the spread paid at purchase and sale, any commissions or platform fees, and the drag from tracking difference if the fund persistently underperforms its benchmark. For a short-term trader, it also includes the likelihood of slippage between the intended price and the executed price. In practice, total cost is not a single number printed in the fund brochure. It is the sum of all the frictions that reduce the return an investor actually keeps. A fund that looks inexpensive on paper can become costly if it is traded poorly or held in a way that magnifies implementation expenses.

This is where investor behavior becomes part of the cost equation. A low-turnover buy-and-hold investor will usually experience different economics from an active trader, even in the same ETF. Someone who invests through periodic contributions may care more about the expense ratio and less about a one-time spread, while someone making tactical shifts may need to focus much more on execution quality. The same fund can be efficient for one investor and inefficient for another, depending on position size, trading frequency, and the liquidity of the market in which it operates. Cost analysis should therefore be tied to usage, not just to product features.

A disciplined comparison usually begins by asking what exposure is needed, then what the fund charges to provide it, and finally what it costs to trade it in practice. Research on passive investing emphasizes that low fees are a major reason these products have grown so quickly, but that same growth has also made it more important to look beyond the headline expense ratio and evaluate how the product is implemented [2] [53]. In ETF selection, the cheapest fund is not automatically the best value. The better question is whether the investor is paying a fair price for the exposure, the trading experience, and the reliability of the result.

Tracking difference and tracking error

Tracking difference is the gap between an ETF's return and the return of the benchmark it is designed to follow. Tracking error is the variability of that gap over time. The two terms are related, but they answer different questions. Tracking difference tells you whether the fund has generally lagged or outperformed its benchmark over a measured period. Tracking error tells you how consistently it has done so. A fund can have a small average shortfall but still show wide swings from month to month, or it can have a modest tracking difference with very steady behavior around the index. For investors, both measures matter because an ETF is often purchased not just for its label, but for the specific exposure it promises to deliver.

The most direct source of tracking difference is cost. Expense ratios, trading expenses inside the portfolio, cash drag, and rebalancing friction all create a return gap between the fund and its benchmark. In some cases, securities lending revenue can offset part of those costs, which is one reason a fund may track better than its headline fee would suggest. Taxes can also affect the result in taxable accounts, especially for funds that realize capital gains or hold assets with less efficient turnover. Even when an ETF is designed to mirror an index closely, the index itself is not investable in a frictionless way. The benchmark may assume instant, costless rebalancing, while the ETF must operate in real markets with spreads, timing delays, and transaction costs.

Tracking error reflects the practical difficulty of replicating the benchmark. It tends to be lower when a fund holds highly liquid securities, uses a straightforward index, and maintains a portfolio that is easy to rebalance. It tends to be higher when the underlying market is less liquid, when the index is concentrated, when the fund uses sampling rather than full replication, or when the strategy is exposed to assets that do not trade continuously. Bond ETFs, for example, may show more tracking variation than broad equity ETFs because many bonds trade infrequently and do not have transparent, continuous pricing. Sector, factor, and thematic ETFs can also exhibit more variation because their underlying holdings may be narrower or more volatile than a broad market benchmark.

It is important not to treat tracking error as a simple measure of quality. A low tracking error is not automatically better if the fund is consistently missing the benchmark in the same direction for structural reasons. Likewise, a slightly higher tracking error may be acceptable if the fund is achieving the intended exposure more efficiently than alternatives. What matters is whether the pattern of deviation is understandable and consistent with the fund's design. An ETF that is built to hold a niche market, use derivatives, or follow a more complex index may naturally have more variation than a plain-vanilla large-cap fund, and that variation is not necessarily a flaw.

Investors should also distinguish between short-term and long-term measurement. Tracking difference can look noisy over a few weeks or months, especially during volatile markets or periods of unusual cash flows. Over a longer horizon, however, persistent underperformance relative to the benchmark becomes more meaningful because small annual gaps compound. That is why it is useful to compare a fund's stated objective with its realized results across multiple periods, not just one recent stretch. A fund that tracks well in calm markets but drifts during stress may not be the right choice for investors who need dependable exposure when conditions change. Passive investors as a group now control substantial market assets, which makes implementation details like these increasingly important for market outcomes as well as portfolio outcomes [2].

The benchmark itself deserves scrutiny. Some indexes are easier to replicate than others, and some are more transparent about their construction, rebalancing rules, and treatment of corporate actions. If an ETF seems to trail its benchmark more than expected, the problem may not be the fund alone; it may also reflect the benchmark's own design. Index methodology can create hidden sources of friction, such as delayed reconstitution, turnover spikes, or concentration in securities that are expensive to trade. In specialized categories, such as ESG or thematic funds, the benchmark may also embed screening rules or selection criteria that alter the portfolio's investability. Research on ESG-related funds and indices has shown that label, methodology, and actual holdings can diverge in ways investors may not assume from the fund name alone [24][26][21].

For that reason, investors should read tracking statistics alongside the fund's structure and purpose. A fund with a very low expense ratio but poor implementation may still disappoint, while a slightly more expensive fund with tighter replication and better execution may deliver better real-world results. The most useful comparison is not just between two ETFs, but between each ETF and the job it is meant to do. If the goal is broad market exposure, then a consistently large tracking gap is a warning sign. If the goal is a specialized allocation, then some deviation may be expected, but it should still be explainable. Tracking difference and tracking error are not abstract academic measures; they are the evidence of how well the ETF wrapper is translating its design into actual investor returns.

Fund size, liquidity, and average trading volume

Fund size, liquidity, and average trading volume are related but not interchangeable measures, and investors benefit from treating them as separate clues rather than as one combined verdict. Fund size usually refers to assets under management, or AUM, which is the total market value of the ETF's holdings. Liquidity is the ease with which shares can be bought or sold without meaningfully affecting price. Average trading volume is the typical number of shares that change hands on an exchange over a given period, usually measured daily. A large fund is often, but not always, easier to trade. A heavily traded fund is often, but not always, the most liquid in the deeper sense that matters to an investor placing an order. The distinction matters because an ETF can have modest daily volume and still trade efficiently if its underlying holdings are liquid and market participants can create or redeem shares smoothly.

Fund size is often used as a quick screen because it gives a rough sense of whether an ETF has attracted meaningful investor interest and whether the sponsor has maintained the product long enough for it to establish a trading record. Larger funds can benefit from economies of scale, and that sometimes supports lower expenses or tighter spreads. Size can also reduce the risk that a fund will be closed simply because it failed to gather assets. Still, size by itself is not a guarantee of quality. A large ETF can be expensive, narrowly focused, or poorly constructed. A smaller ETF can be perfectly usable if it tracks a liquid market and has a sensible structure. In other words, size is a useful stability signal, not a substitute for evaluating what the fund actually owns and how it trades.

Average trading volume is the most visible liquidity measure because it is easy to see on a quote screen, but it can be misleading if taken in isolation. A fund with low reported volume may still be easy to trade when its underlying securities are highly liquid and market makers are active. That is because ETF shares are not limited to the shares that happened to trade earlier in the day. Authorized participants can create or redeem shares in the primary market, which helps keep supply aligned with demand. For broad, well-known equity ETFs, the exchange volume may understate true trading capacity. For funds holding less liquid assets, however, volume becomes more important because the market may need to work harder to absorb larger orders without moving the price.

Liquidity also has several layers. There is the liquidity of the ETF shares themselves, the liquidity of the underlying portfolio, and the liquidity available through the market-making and creation-redemption process. An ETF that holds large-cap U.S. stocks may be easier to trade than a fund with the same daily volume that holds thinly traded bonds, frontier-market securities, or niche thematic exposures. This is why a low-volume ETF is not automatically a problem, and why a high-volume ETF is not automatically safe from trading friction. The real question is whether the fund can be bought or sold in the size and time frame the investor needs, at a cost that remains reasonable relative to the position size.

For most individual investors, the practical issue is not whether an ETF trades millions of shares per day, but whether the order can be executed cleanly. A small purchase in a broad-market ETF may be perfectly fine even if volume is only moderate, because the bid-ask spread is narrow and the underlying market is deep. A larger trade, or a trade in a specialized ETF, deserves more care. Investors should pay attention to the spread, the time of day, and whether the market is calm or stressed. During volatile periods, even liquid ETFs can show wider spreads, and that can matter more than the fund's headline volume. In that setting, the cost of impatience may exceed the apparent savings from choosing the "most popular" fund.

It is also useful to think about liquidity in relation to portfolio size. An ETF that is perfectly adequate for a small position may not be ideal for a large allocation, particularly if the fund is concentrated in less liquid securities. As position size grows, the investor becomes more sensitive to market impact, spreads, and the possibility that the ETF's price can move away from its underlying value during periods of stress. That is one reason institutional investors and advisers often look beyond the ticker's trading activity and examine the depth of the underlying market. Research on capital flows and benchmark behavior has shown that large allocations can cluster around widely followed products and reference points [25], which helps explain why some ETFs become especially central to trading and portfolio implementation.

There is no single cutoff that defines an acceptable fund size or volume threshold for every investor. A broad U.S. equity ETF with enormous assets and heavy trading may be ideal for one purpose, while a more specialized fund with modest volume may still be appropriate for another. The better approach is to ask whether the ETF's size supports its strategy, whether the underlying market is liquid enough for the intended use, and whether the trading activity is sufficient for the order you plan to place. In practice, that means using size, liquidity, and average trading volume together as a screening framework rather than as a checklist of isolated numbers. The goal is not to find the biggest ETF, but the one whose trading profile matches the role it is meant to play in the portfolio.

Index methodology, holdings transparency, and fund provider reputation

An ETF's index methodology is the blueprint behind its behavior. The benchmark does not merely name the fund; it defines what belongs in the portfolio, how securities are weighted, how often the portfolio changes, and what kinds of companies or bonds are allowed to enter or leave. Two funds can both say they track "the market" and still differ materially if one uses a broad, capitalization-weighted index while another applies screens for profitability, volatility, dividends, or ESG characteristics. That difference matters because the index is where many of the fund's risks, biases, and costs are embedded before the first share is ever traded. Research on index investing has shown that benchmark design is far from uniform and that the same general label can conceal substantial variation in construction rules [10]. For investors, the practical question is not whether an ETF tracks an index, but what kind of index it tracks and how that index is maintained.

Methodology deserves close attention because it affects exposure, turnover, and implementation quality. A market-cap-weighted index will naturally give the largest companies the biggest influence, which may be appropriate for a core portfolio but may also concentrate exposure in a small number of dominant names or sectors. Equal-weighted or factor-based indexes spread influence differently and can create a distinct return pattern, but they may require more frequent rebalancing and can be more sensitive to market swings. Some indexes use screens based on size, liquidity, profitability, momentum, or sustainability criteria, and each screen changes the investable universe in ways that are not always obvious from the ETF's marketing name. In practice, the index rulebook should answer several basic questions: How are securities selected? How are they weighted? How often is the index reconstituted or rebalanced? What happens when a security no longer meets the criteria? The more clearly those rules are defined, the easier it is to understand what the ETF is actually trying to own.

Holdings transparency is the other side of that equation. Because ETFs trade intraday, investors often assume they know what they own simply by looking at the ticker and the latest price. In reality, the quality and frequency of disclosure vary. Many ETFs publish full holdings daily, which allows investors, advisers, and market participants to see the portfolio with a high degree of precision. Others disclose less frequently or provide only a representative sample, especially in strategies that are designed to protect proprietary trading methods. For transparent funds, this visibility helps investors evaluate overlap, concentration, sector exposure, and tax-related behavior. It also makes it easier to compare the fund's actual holdings with its stated objective. When disclosure is limited, that comparison becomes harder, and the investor must rely more heavily on the sponsor's reputation, the precision of the index rules, and the fund's historical behavior. Transparency is not automatically a virtue in every context, but it is an important part of due diligence because it allows the market to discipline the product more effectively [4].

There is also a difference between knowing the names of the holdings and understanding how faithfully those holdings reflect the stated strategy. A fund may disclose its portfolio and still leave room for surprises if the benchmark itself is complex or if the strategy depends on discretionary judgment. This is especially relevant in ESG and thematic ETFs, where the underlying definitions can vary widely across providers. Studies of ESG investing have noted that different metrics and methodologies can produce markedly different results even when funds use similar language [54]. That same issue extends beyond ESG to many specialty ETFs: the label may be broad, but the implementation can be narrow, selective, or heavily dependent on the sponsor's interpretation. For that reason, holdings transparency should be read together with methodology. A transparent portfolio is easier to inspect, but a clear methodology is what tells you whether the portfolio is built in a way that matches the stated objective.

Fund provider reputation matters because the sponsor is responsible for the design, oversight, and operational consistency of the ETF. In an industry that is large, diverse, and uneven in data quality, sponsor quality is not a trivial matter [15]. A reputable provider is more likely to maintain disciplined index governance, manage rebalancing and corporate actions carefully, communicate changes clearly, and support the fund through periods of stress. This does not mean that large sponsors are always better or that smaller sponsors are always inferior. It does mean that investors should look for evidence of competence and consistency: how long the provider has operated ETFs, whether it has a record in the asset class, how it handles closures or mergers, how clearly it explains methodology changes, and whether it has shown an ability to preserve investor interests when market conditions are difficult. In passive strategies, the sponsor's role may appear limited, but the literature on passive investing emphasizes that these funds are powerful market actors and that their governance and engagement choices still matter [2].

Reputation is especially important when a fund uses a less familiar construction process or a less liquid underlying market. A provider offering a conventional large-cap equity ETF has a different challenge than one launching an ETF tied to corporate bonds, emerging markets, or a niche thematic index. In harder-to-trade markets, operational skill and index governance can have a larger effect on results than the headline expense ratio suggests. Investors should therefore treat the provider as part of the product itself. A low fee is useful, but it is not a substitute for a sponsor that can manage sampling, creation and redemption activity, index changes, and disclosure practices with care. When the methodology is complicated and the holdings are not fully visible every day, the sponsor's track record becomes more important, not less.

CHAPTER 5

Chapter 5: Aligning ETFs with Investment Goals

Once an investor moves from identifying an ETF to deciding whether it belongs in a portfolio, the question shifts from product features to purpose. A fund that looks attractive in isolation may be poorly suited to the role it is expected to play if its risk profile, liquidity, or underlying exposure does not align with the investor's objectives. That alignment begins with a clear view of what the money is meant to accomplish, how long it can remain invested, and how much uncertainty the investor can realistically accept along the way.

Defining goals, time horizon, and risk tolerance

Before selecting an ETF, an investor should define the role the position is meant to play. That role is shaped by three related questions: what the money is for, when it will be needed, and how much uncertainty the investor can tolerate along the way. A fund can be excellent in the abstract and still be a poor fit if it is being asked to do the wrong job. A long-term retirement account, a down payment reserve, and a source of portfolio income all call for different combinations of growth potential, stability, and liquidity. The point is not to find the "best" ETF in isolation, but the one whose structure matches the account's purpose.

Goals should be specific enough to guide implementation. "Build wealth" is too broad to be useful by itself, while "accumulate $250,000 for retirement over 20 years" or "preserve capital for a home purchase in five years" gives the portfolio a clearer assignment. The more precise the objective, the easier it becomes to choose between a broad equity ETF, a bond ETF, a cash-like fund, or a more specialized strategy. Investors often underestimate how much the intended use of the money should influence the choice of risk level. A fund that is appropriate for a decades-long retirement horizon may be far too volatile for a goal that is only a few years away.

Time horizon is one of the most important filters in ETF selection because it determines how much temporary loss the investor can absorb without being forced to sell. A long horizon allows more room for equity exposure and for strategies that may experience sharp drawdowns before recovering. A shorter horizon usually calls for greater caution, because the investor has less time to wait out a decline. This is not simply a matter of emotional comfort; it is a matter of sequence risk. If money will be needed soon, a large market drop can permanently change the outcome by forcing liquidation at an unfavorable time. The closer the goal, the more the portfolio should emphasize capital preservation and predictable liquidity.

Risk tolerance is related to time horizon but not identical to it. Two investors with the same long-term goal may react very differently to volatility, and those differences matter because a portfolio is only useful if the investor can actually stay with it. Risk tolerance includes the ability to endure short-term losses, the willingness to accept volatility in exchange for potential growth, and the discipline to avoid changing course at the wrong moment. It is also shaped by income stability, other assets, debt obligations, and psychological comfort with uncertainty. A person with a steady paycheck and no near-term liabilities may be able to tolerate more market fluctuation than someone who depends on portfolio withdrawals or has limited savings outside the investment account.

In practice, risk tolerance should be treated as a constraint rather than an aspiration. Many investors say they want aggressive growth until they experience their first major decline. At that point, the portfolio may suddenly feel too risky, and the result can be selling at the wrong time. A better approach is to choose an allocation that is sustainable through uncomfortable periods, not just attractive during calm markets. Passive investing has become dominant in large part because it combines low cost with broad diversification [53], but diversification does not eliminate the need to size risk appropriately. Even a well-diversified ETF portfolio can decline materially if it is concentrated in equities or in a narrow segment of the market.

These three factors should be considered together. A long horizon may justify more risk, but only if the goal and the investor's behavior support it. A short horizon may require conservative positioning even if the investor is comfortable with volatility, because the calendar itself limits recovery time. The result is a practical balance: growth-oriented ETFs for money that can remain invested for many years, more defensive ETFs for capital that must be available sooner, and a mix of exposures when the account serves multiple purposes. For investors who are building a portfolio from the ground up, the objective is not to maximize excitement or minimize every fluctuation; it is to align the ETF with the role the capital is expected to play.

It also helps to distinguish between the return target and the acceptable path to that return. Two portfolios may aim for similar long-term outcomes, yet one may reach them through a smoother pattern of gains and losses while the other relies on greater volatility. That path matters because investors experience the journey, not just the endpoint. When selecting ETFs, this means looking beyond headline performance and asking whether the fund's underlying exposure is compatible with the account's purpose. In a market where product choice is abundant and increasingly refined, disciplined goal-setting becomes a form of risk management in its own right [15].

Using ETFs for long-term wealth building

For long-term wealth building, the central advantage of ETFs is not that they promise unusually high returns, but that they make it easier to stay invested in a disciplined, diversified, and cost-conscious way. Over long periods, portfolio results are shaped less by any single trade than by the interaction of asset allocation, fees, taxes, and investor behavior. ETFs fit that framework well because they provide broad market exposure in a form that is simple to hold, easy to rebalance, and generally inexpensive to maintain. That combination matters most when the goal is not to outperform in a single year, but to compound capital steadily across many years.

A long-term ETF portfolio usually works best when the funds serve clear roles. A broad equity ETF can act as a growth engine, a bond ETF can provide ballast, and an international ETF can reduce reliance on a single economy or currency. The point is not to collect as many funds as possible, but to assemble exposures that work together. Because ETFs are transparent, an investor can see what is owned, how much overlap exists, and whether the portfolio is unintentionally concentrated in a few large companies or sectors. That clarity supports better decisions over time, especially when the market environment changes and the temptation to make reactive shifts increases.

Cost control is especially important in a long horizon strategy because small annual differences compound. A lower expense ratio leaves more of the market's return in the investor's account, and reduced turnover can also help limit unnecessary trading frictions. This is one reason passive funds have become so influential in modern markets: they channel capital efficiently and at scale, while giving investors a straightforward way to participate in broad market growth [2]. For long-term wealth building, the goal is not to find the cheapest fund in isolation, but to avoid paying more than is necessary for the exposure being sought. When two ETFs provide similar market access, the one with lower ongoing drag often has the advantage simply because compounding works on the net return, not the gross one.

Tax treatment also matters, particularly in taxable accounts. ETFs are often used because their structure can support tax efficiency relative to some other pooled vehicles, though the actual outcome depends on the fund, the asset class, and the investor's own situation [48]. For a long-term investor, this means attention should be paid not only to the stated strategy, but also to how distributions are handled, how often the fund turns over holdings, and whether the position belongs in a taxable account or a retirement account. A fund that looks attractive before tax can become less compelling after distributions and trading costs are considered. Long-term wealth building is therefore not just about return potential; it is also about keeping more of what the market generates.

Behavioral discipline is another area where ETFs are useful. Because they trade during the day, they can tempt investors into frequent trading, but their real strength for long-term compounding comes from being held through market cycles rather than traded around them. A portfolio built with ETFs can be rebalanced periodically without constant intervention, allowing the investor to maintain target allocations while avoiding the noise of daily headlines. This is especially important because long-term results are often damaged less by poor fund selection than by repeated attempts to time entries and exits. ETFs make it easy to act, but that same ease should be matched with a clear plan for when action is actually warranted.

The long-term case for ETFs becomes even stronger when the investor's objectives are connected to broader structural trends in markets. As capital increasingly flows through passive vehicles, ETFs have become a major force in asset allocation and corporate ownership [2]. At the same time, the growth of specialized strategies, including ESG and thematic funds, has raised the importance of understanding what is actually inside the wrapper and how index design influences outcomes [4][21]. For wealth building, this reinforces a simple principle: use ETFs to capture durable exposures, not just fashionable narratives. A fund should be chosen because it supports a portfolio role that can be defended over many years, not because it is currently popular.

In practice, long-term ETF investing works best when the portfolio is built around patience, consistency, and fit. Regular contributions, periodic rebalancing, and a willingness to hold through volatility often matter more than elaborate strategy changes. The investor who uses ETFs to stay broadly diversified, keep costs contained, and avoid unnecessary turnover is already using the structure in the way it was designed to be used. That is what makes ETFs especially effective for wealth building over time: they reduce many of the obstacles that prevent investors from capturing the market's long-run compounding while preserving enough flexibility to adapt as goals and circumstances evolve.

Using ETFs for income, stability, and tactical allocation

ETFs can serve roles that go beyond simple market exposure, and those roles often matter most when an investor is trying to solve a specific portfolio problem rather than merely add another holding. For income, the appeal is usually the ability to turn part of a portfolio into a regular cash-flow stream without giving up the diversification and tradability of a fund structure. For stability, the objective is less about maximizing return and more about dampening volatility, preserving purchasing power, and providing a source of ballast when equity markets are under stress. For tactical allocation, the ETF is a tool for making a deliberate, time-sensitive shift in exposure without needing to rebuild a portfolio from individual securities. In each case, the fund is being used as an implementation vehicle, and the investor should judge it by how well it performs that role.

Income-oriented ETF use starts with understanding where the cash flow comes from. In equity ETFs, distributions may reflect dividends from underlying companies. In bond ETFs, income is generated primarily from coupon payments, adjusted for the fund's expenses, trading activity, and the current level of interest rates. Some ETFs are designed to emphasize higher current yield, but yield alone is not a complete measure of usefulness. A fund can advertise an attractive distribution rate while carrying hidden tradeoffs such as lower credit quality, longer duration, greater concentration, or exposure to sectors that are more vulnerable in a downturn. Investors should therefore distinguish between income and yield chasing. A higher payout is not automatically better if it comes with a level of risk that is inconsistent with the portfolio's purpose.

The structure of the income stream also matters. Some investors want monthly distributions to match spending needs, while others may prefer quarterly payouts because they are more typical of the underlying securities. The frequency of distributions can be convenient, but it should not be confused with total return. An ETF that pays income regularly may still lose value if its holdings decline or if rising rates pressure the price of the underlying assets. This is especially relevant in bond ETFs, where duration and credit quality shape both income and price sensitivity. A short-duration bond ETF may offer lower yield than a longer-duration fund, but it may also be less vulnerable when interest rates rise. The right choice depends on whether the investor is trying to generate spendable cash, reduce volatility, or hold a temporary parking place for capital.

Stability is often sought through fixed income, short-duration instruments, and broad, less concentrated equity exposure. Bond ETFs are commonly used because they can provide a diversified way to hold government, corporate, or municipal debt without having to buy and monitor individual issues. Their usefulness is partly practical: they can be traded easily, sized precisely, and adjusted quickly as conditions change. But stability should not be mistaken for immunity. Bond ETFs still move in response to interest rates, credit spreads, and liquidity conditions, and some segments can be more volatile than investors expect. Corporate bond exposure, for example, may behave differently from Treasuries during periods of stress, and lower-quality credit can lose defensive value when markets become risk-averse. Research on benchmark design and portfolio implementation has long emphasized that the reference exposure itself matters as much as the wrapper around it [11].

In a broader portfolio context, stability can also come from using ETFs to diversify across asset classes and regions. A portfolio that is heavily concentrated in one country, one sector, or one style may appear diversified because it holds many securities, but it can still be exposed to a common risk driver. Broad market ETFs, high-quality bond ETFs, and cash-equivalent ETFs can help reduce that concentration. Commodity ETFs are sometimes considered as a diversifying sleeve as well, although their behavior can be uneven and their role should be defined carefully. Academic reviews note that commodities have been used for their distinct return drivers and hedging characteristics, but they are not a substitute for core portfolio diversification [49]. The point is not that every stabilizing ETF must be low volatility in all environments; it is that the fund should contribute a different risk profile than the assets already in the portfolio.

Tactical allocation uses ETFs differently. Instead of being held mainly for long-term strategic exposure, they can be used to express a shorter-term view on markets, sectors, factors, regions, or asset classes. This may involve increasing equity exposure when the investor believes risk assets are attractively priced, reducing duration when interest rates appear likely to rise, or adding a sector ETF to reflect a view about earnings momentum or policy trends. The advantage of using ETFs for this purpose is implementation speed. A position can be established or reduced quickly, with transparency and without the operational burden of trading many individual holdings. That said, tactical use raises the bar for discipline. If the thesis is weak, vague, or constantly changing, the ETF becomes a convenient way to overtrade rather than a precise tool for portfolio adjustment.

Because tactical allocation is often driven by shorter time horizons, liquidity and trading costs deserve special attention. A fund that is excellent for strategic holding may still be a poor tactical instrument if its spread is wide, its underlying market is thin, or its price tends to deviate from net asset value during active sessions. This is especially true in less liquid segments such as emerging markets, specialized credit, or niche thematic exposures, where the implementation cost can be larger than the headline expense ratio suggests. Research on emerging-market investment vehicles has highlighted how low liquidity and limited diversification can constrain portfolio construction and risk control [80]. Tactical decisions should therefore be made with full awareness of not only the intended market view, but also the cost of entering and exiting the position.

For all three uses, the central question is fit. An income ETF should support spending or distribution needs without introducing an unacceptable level of hidden risk. A stability ETF should lower overall portfolio volatility or provide a reserve of defensiveness that behaves as expected when other assets are under pressure. A tactical ETF should translate a market view into a controlled position size, with clear entry and exit logic. The same fund may be useful in one role and unsuitable in another. Investors who separate the ETF's function from its label are better positioned to choose exposures that serve the portfolio instead of merely adding another line item to it.

Matching ETF selection to personal financial priorities

Matching ETF selection to personal financial priorities starts with recognizing that "best" is not a universal label. The most suitable ETF is the one that fits the role a position is meant to play in a broader financial life. A retiree drawing income, a young worker building long-term wealth, and a household preserving capital for a planned expense all have different priorities, even if they are looking at the same menu of funds. The right selection process begins by translating those priorities into portfolio requirements: growth, income, stability, tax efficiency, simplicity, or some combination of the four.

When growth is the main objective, investors usually benefit from keeping the emphasis on broad, low-cost exposures that can compound over time without requiring constant intervention. In that setting, the question is less about finding the ETF with the highest recent return and more about choosing a fund that offers durable market exposure at a reasonable cost. A portfolio built around broad equity ETFs can support long horizons because it gives the investor participation in economic growth while reducing the need to predict which sector, country, or style will lead next. That approach also tends to be easier to maintain through market cycles, which matters because long-term success depends heavily on staying invested. Research on mutual fund outcomes has shown how difficult it can be for many actively managed vehicles to consistently beat broad market benchmarks over time [83], which reinforces the appeal of simple, rules-based ETF exposure when the priority is accumulation rather than short-term outperformance.

If income is the priority, ETF selection should focus on the source, reliability, and tradeoffs of that income stream. A yield number alone does not tell the whole story. Investors need to know whether distributions are coming from dividends, interest, option premiums, or a mix of sources, because each has different implications for volatility, tax treatment, and sustainability. A higher yield can sometimes reflect greater underlying risk rather than better cash flow. For example, a fund concentrated in lower-quality credit or highly cyclical dividend payers may look attractive on a distribution screen but behave poorly when markets weaken. Income-oriented investors therefore need to think in terms of portfolio function: is the ETF meant to supplement spending, reduce the need to sell shares, or provide a steadier stream during retirement? The answer influences whether a bond ETF, dividend equity ETF, preferred securities ETF, or a more conservative multi-asset fund is the better fit.

For investors prioritizing stability, the selection process should place more weight on drawdown behavior and underlying asset sensitivity than on headline return. Stability-oriented ETFs are often used to reduce portfolio swings, preserve capital for near-term needs, or provide a buffer against more volatile holdings. In practice, that means examining duration, credit quality, sector concentration, and equity sensitivity rather than simply assuming that a bond ETF or defensive equity ETF will behave gently in all environments. A short-duration bond ETF may be more suitable than a long-duration fund when the investor is worried about rate volatility. A high-quality, broad fixed-income ETF may be preferable to a narrow credit fund if the goal is capital preservation. The key is to match the ETF's risk drivers to the investor's tolerance for short-term fluctuations and the time frame over which the money may be needed.

Tax considerations also belong in the priority-setting process, especially for investors holding ETFs in taxable accounts. Two funds with similar market exposure can produce different after-tax outcomes depending on turnover, distribution patterns, and the nature of the underlying holdings. A tax-aware investor may prefer a broad market ETF with low turnover over a more active strategy that generates frequent realized gains. In some cases, the best ETF is not the one with the most attractive pre-tax profile, but the one that preserves more of the return after taxes. This is one reason portfolio context matters so much: an ETF that is efficient in a retirement account may not be the same ETF that makes the most sense in a taxable account. The structure of the account can be as important as the structure of the fund.

Simplicity is another legitimate priority, and it often leads investors toward a smaller number of core holdings rather than a large collection of specialized products. A simple portfolio can be easier to understand, easier to rebalance, and less likely to tempt the investor into unnecessary trading. That does not mean simplicity requires sacrificing precision. It means choosing ETFs that cover the needed exposures cleanly, with minimal overlap and little ambiguity about what they own. Investors who value simplicity should be cautious about adding thematic or narrowly focused ETFs unless those funds solve a clearly defined problem. The more specialized the fund, the more likely it is to introduce hidden complexity in the form of concentration, style drift, or performance that depends on a very specific market environment.

Personal priorities also change over time, and ETF selection should change with them. A portfolio built for accumulation in the early working years may shift toward income and stability as retirement approaches. A family saving for college may need a glide path that gradually reduces volatility as the spending date nears. Even within the same investor's life, priorities can move with job changes, market conditions, tax brackets, and household obligations. That is why ETF selection should be treated as an ongoing alignment exercise rather than a one-time purchase decision. The most useful question is not simply whether a fund is good, but whether it is still serving the purpose for which it was selected.

A disciplined way to make that judgment is to rank priorities before comparing funds. If growth outranks income, the investor should not let a higher yield distract from a weaker long-term structure. If stability outranks return, the investor should not accept extra volatility merely because a fund has recently outperformed. If tax efficiency outranks simplicity, the investor may need to accept a slightly more nuanced portfolio design. The ETF industry offers enough variety that most investors can find funds suited to their objectives, but the burden remains on the investor to define those objectives clearly. Once that is done, selection becomes a matter of fit rather than fascination, and the role of each ETF in the portfolio becomes much easier to defend when markets stop behaving calmly.

CHAPTER 7

Chapter 7: Risk Management for ETF Investors

Risk management is where ETF investing becomes less about choosing attractive products and more about understanding how those products behave when conditions change. A fund can be well designed, low cost, and easy to trade, yet still expose a portfolio to losses that are larger or more persistent than the investor expected. The main task here is to identify the sources of risk that sit inside the ETF itself, the risks that arise from how it is used in a portfolio, and the risks that come from the investor's own response to market stress.

Market risk, interest rate risk, and credit risk

Market risk is the broadest risk an ETF investor faces because it comes from the market itself rather than from the fund wrapper. If stock prices fall across the board, an equity ETF will usually decline with them, even when the fund is highly diversified and efficiently managed. The same logic applies to bond ETFs when rates rise or credit conditions worsen. An ETF can reduce security-specific risk by spreading holdings across many issuers, but it cannot eliminate the possibility that the entire asset class moves against the investor. That distinction matters because diversification is often misunderstood as protection from loss, when in practice it is mainly a way to reduce the damage caused by any single holding.

For equity ETFs, market risk is tied to the economic and psychological forces that drive share prices: earnings expectations, interest rates, inflation, growth fears, and investor sentiment. A broad market fund may look stable in ordinary periods, but it will still experience drawdowns when the overall equity market re-prices. Sector and thematic ETFs can magnify that effect because they concentrate exposure in a narrower slice of the market. If technology leads the market higher, a tech-heavy ETF may outperform; if the cycle turns, the same concentration can intensify losses. The important point is that market risk is not a flaw in the ETF structure. It is the price of owning the underlying asset class.

Interest rate risk is most visible in bond ETFs, where changes in rates directly affect prices. When prevailing interest rates rise, the market value of existing bonds generally falls because newer bonds can offer higher yields. The reverse is also true: when rates decline, existing bonds with higher coupons may become more valuable. Bond ETFs translate that relationship into daily market pricing. The degree of sensitivity depends on duration, which measures how strongly a bond or bond portfolio tends to react to rate changes. Longer-duration ETFs usually have more price volatility than shorter-duration funds because their cash flows are farther in the future and therefore more exposed to discount-rate changes. This is why two bond ETFs can both be "fixed income" and yet behave very differently in a rising-rate environment.

Duration is only part of the picture. Yield curve shifts can affect segments of the bond market differently, and an ETF's maturity profile can shape how it responds. A short-term Treasury ETF may hold up relatively well when rates move higher, while a long-term Treasury ETF can experience a much larger decline. Investors sometimes assume that bonds are safe simply because they are less volatile than stocks over long periods, but that assumption can be misleading in the short run. A bond

ETF is still a market instrument, and its price reflects changing expectations about inflation, policy, and future yields. For investors using bond ETFs as a stabilizing allocation, matching duration to the portfolio's purpose is therefore essential.

Credit risk is the risk that a bond issuer will fail to meet its obligations or that the market will reassess the issuer's ability to do so. In ETF form, this risk shows up most clearly in funds that own corporate bonds, high-yield bonds, bank loans, or other securities tied to the financial health of borrowers. When credit conditions are calm, yield spreads may be narrow and credit ETFs can appear steady. When economic stress rises, those spreads can widen quickly, pushing prices lower even if interest rates themselves are unchanged. In other words, a credit ETF may decline because the market is demanding more compensation for default risk, not because the rate environment has changed. That distinction helps explain why credit-sensitive ETFs often behave more like risk assets than like traditional defensive holdings.

Credit quality matters because not all bond ETFs carry the same kind of exposure. A fund concentrated in investment-grade issuers generally faces lower default risk than a high-yield fund, but it may still be vulnerable to spread widening if investors become more cautious. A diversified bond ETF may hold dozens or hundreds of issuers, yet it can still be exposed to common credit pressures if those issuers belong to the same sector, region, or economic cycle. During periods of stress, credit risk can interact with liquidity risk as market participants become less willing to trade lower-quality bonds at stable prices. The fund may continue to function, but the market price can move sharply as investors reassess the probability of repayment.

For ETF investors, the practical challenge is not to avoid these risks entirely, because that is not possible, but to understand which risks are embedded in each fund and whether they fit the role the fund is meant to play. A broad equity ETF may be appropriate as a long-term growth holding precisely because it accepts market risk in exchange for participation in the equity premium. A short-duration bond ETF may be used to reduce interest rate sensitivity, while an investment-grade credit ETF may be chosen for income with moderate credit exposure. The key is to read the ETF's underlying exposure, not just its label. Two funds can both be described as conservative or diversified and still respond very differently when markets reprice, rates shift, or borrowers weaken. That is why risk analysis begins with the assets inside the ETF, not with the exchange-traded wrapper itself.

Sector concentration and factor exposure risk

Sector concentration risk arises when an ETF's holdings are clustered in a relatively small part of the economy, so that portfolio results become heavily dependent on the fortunes of one industry or a handful of related industries. A sector fund can be useful when an investor wants targeted exposure, but that same focus also means the fund is less forgiving if the sector falls out of favor. An ETF tied to technology, financials, energy, health care, or semiconductors may still hold many securities, yet those holdings can move together because they respond to the same drivers: regulation, interest rates, commodity prices, capital spending, consumer demand, or innovation cycles. The diversification inside the fund is therefore narrower than the share count might suggest. This is one reason broad passive investing has grown so quickly: investors often want low cost and diversification at the same time, and concentrated sector bets do not provide the same balance [53].

The key issue is not whether a sector is "good" or "bad," but whether the investor understands how much of the portfolio's outcome is being assigned to one part of the market. A sector ETF can outperform dramatically during a favorable cycle, and that success can make the

the most efficient first step because it reduces trading costs and may avoid taxable gains in taxable accounts. For example, if equities have grown above target and bonds have fallen below it, fresh cash can be used to buy bond ETFs instead of adding to stocks. This method is especially useful for investors who are still accumulating assets. It keeps the portfolio moving back toward its target without forcing constant liquidation of appreciated positions.

Tax location and account type should also shape the maintenance process. In taxable accounts, selling an ETF may create capital gains, so the cost of rebalancing is not limited to commissions or bid-ask spreads. A portfolio that is slightly off target may be better left alone if the tax bill would outweigh the benefit of immediate adjustment. In retirement accounts, where trades do not trigger current taxes in the same way, rebalancing can usually be done more freely. This is one reason investors often maintain a more active rebalancing discipline inside tax-advantaged accounts while using cash flows and wider bands in taxable accounts.

The same logic applies to portfolio maintenance more broadly. Rebalancing is not only about restoring percentages; it is also about checking whether the portfolio still reflects the investor's actual situation. A change in income, time horizon, savings rate, or risk tolerance may justify a new target allocation rather than a simple trade back to the old one. In that sense, maintenance is partly mechanical and partly supervisory. The mechanical side keeps the weights in line. The supervisory side asks whether the weights themselves still make sense. Research on asset allocation emphasizes that disciplined capital allocation is central to long-term efficiency and portfolio effectiveness [81], which is why rebalancing should be treated as part of an ongoing management process rather than an occasional cleanup task.

CHAPTER 6

Chapter 6: Building a Diversified ETF Portfolio

Once the building blocks of ETF selection are in place, the next task is to combine them into a portfolio that does more than simply hold several funds at once. Diversification is not achieved by adding symbols mechanically; it comes from arranging exposures so that each holding serves a distinct purpose and the overall mix behaves coherently across different market environments. That requires thinking in terms of roles, relationships, and tradeoffs rather than isolated product features. A portfolio can lean toward simplicity or precision, toward broad market coverage or deliberate tilts, but it should still reflect a clear structure that connects the investor's objectives to the assets being used.

Core-satellite portfolio design

Core-satellite design begins with a simple portfolio rule: use one set of holdings to provide the durable, long-term exposure you want to own through most market conditions, and use a second set to express narrower convictions without allowing those convictions to dominate the portfolio. In ETF terms, the core is usually built from broad, low-cost funds that cover the main return drivers of the market, while the satellites are smaller positions that add targeted exposures, tilts, or specialized strategies. The distinction is less about labels than about function. A core holding should be dependable, diversified, and easy to maintain. A

satellite holding should be deliberate, limited in size, and chosen for a specific reason.

The core is the part of the portfolio that does the heavy lifting. For many investors, that means a broad equity ETF or a combination of broad equity and bond ETFs that together establish the portfolio's baseline risk and return profile. Because the core is meant to be held for long periods, it is usually better to favor simplicity, liquidity, and transparency over novelty. The purpose is not to find the most exciting fund, but the one that gives the clearest exposure to the market segment you want in the largest proportion. This is where broad diversification matters most, because the core should reduce the need to make repeated decisions about individual sectors, themes, or market stories.

The satellite sleeve serves a different purpose. It can be used to express a view on a region, sector, factor, or theme; to adjust the portfolio's income profile; or to add a specific risk exposure that is not fully captured by the core. A satellite allocation may include a small-cap ETF, a value tilt, an international emerging markets fund, a bond fund with a different duration profile, or a thematic ETF tied to a long-term trend. The key is that satellites should be additions, not substitutes for the portfolio's foundation. They are most useful when the investor can explain why the exposure is being added, what role it is meant to play, and what would make it worth holding through periods of underperformance.

Size discipline is what keeps the structure from turning into a collection of unrelated ideas. If satellites become too large, the portfolio starts to behave less like a diversified core with intentional tilts and more like a set of concentrated bets. That can be acceptable for an investor with a strong conviction and a long horizon, but it changes the character of the portfolio and increases the chance that short-term disappointment will lead to poor decisions. A smaller satellite allocation helps preserve

the core's role as the anchor while still giving room for active judgment. The exact percentage depends on the investor's experience, risk tolerance, and purpose, but the principle remains the same: the core should remain dominant enough that the portfolio's long-term behavior is still driven primarily by broad market exposure.

Core-satellite design also helps separate strategic decisions from tactical ones. The core represents the long-run policy allocation, the part of the portfolio that should change only when the investor's goals, time horizon, or risk tolerance change. Satellites can be used more flexibly, but that flexibility should not be confused with frequency. A satellite position is not automatically a trading vehicle. It can be held for years if the underlying thesis remains intact. The advantage of the structure is that it gives the investor a place to express conviction without disturbing the rest of the portfolio every time a new idea appears. In that sense, the design supports discipline by making the boundary between permanent and provisional capital explicit.

Implementation matters because a poor choice of core can undermine the entire structure. A core holding that is too narrow, too costly, or too complex will force the satellites to do work they were never meant to do. Likewise, a satellite chosen only because it has recently outperformed can create hidden overlap with the core or introduce risks that are not obvious from the fund's name. An investor may think a satellite adds diversification when it actually increases concentration in the same stocks, sectors, or factors already present in the core. Careful review of holdings, benchmark construction, and factor exposure is therefore essential. Benchmark design is not a minor detail; it shapes what the portfolio really owns [92].

Core-satellite portfolios are especially useful because they combine two different strengths of ETF investing: efficient access to broad markets and precise access to narrower exposures. That combination is

valuable, but only when the roles are kept distinct. The core should be selected for durability and cost efficiency. The satellites should be selected for a clear thesis and a defined size. When those roles are respected, the portfolio can remain stable enough for long-term compounding while still allowing room for judgment, adaptation, and selective opportunity. In practice, the structure is less about predicting the future than about organizing uncertainty in a way that is easier to manage.

Asset allocation across stocks, bonds, and alternatives

Asset allocation is the part of portfolio construction that determines where the portfolio's risk and return are expected to come from. With ETFs, that decision is unusually transparent because the fund lineup makes the major building blocks visible: stocks for growth, bonds for income and stability, and alternatives for exposures that do not fit neatly into either category. The point is not to own every category in equal measure. It is to combine them in proportions that reflect the investor's time horizon, spending needs, tolerance for volatility, and willingness to accept periods when one asset class is clearly out of favor.

Stocks are typically the primary engine of long-term growth. Equity ETFs can provide broad exposure to the market as a whole, or they can narrow the focus to regions, sectors, styles, or dividend characteristics. In an asset allocation framework, the equity sleeve is usually where an investor accepts the most price fluctuation in exchange for the possibility of higher long-run returns. That makes the stock allocation especially important for investors with long horizons, because the ability to remain invested through downturns often matters more than trying to predict the next market move. The exact mix within equities can vary, but the broad idea remains the same: stocks supply growth, and the portfolio must be

sized so that the investor can tolerate their volatility without abandoning the plan.

Bonds serve a different role. They are commonly used to moderate portfolio swings, provide potential income, and create a source of capital that may hold up better than equities during periods of market stress. Bond ETFs make it possible to express that role with precision, whether the goal is short duration, intermediate duration, inflation protection, or credit exposure. But bonds are not a single risk bucket. Interest rate risk, credit risk, and maturity all matter, and a bond ETF can behave very differently depending on those choices. A portfolio that includes bonds for stability should therefore distinguish between bonds that are likely to cushion equity declines and bonds that may be more sensitive to rate changes or credit spreads. In other words, the label "bond ETF" does not guarantee conservatism; the underlying exposure determines how defensive the allocation really is.

Alternatives occupy a more specialized place. In ETF portfolios, this category can include commodities, real assets, precious metals, infrastructure, and other exposures that are intended to behave differently from traditional stocks and bonds. Their value is often tied to a specific economic driver, such as inflation, supply constraints, or resource demand, rather than to broad corporate earnings or bond yields. Research on commodities has shown that they can offer diversification benefits under certain conditions, although those benefits are not uniform across time or market regimes [9]. That makes alternatives useful as diversifiers, but not as substitutes for a disciplined core. They are generally most effective when used selectively and with a clear purpose, rather than as a large allocation added simply because the category sounds sophisticated.

The right balance among these three sleeves depends on the investor's objective. A younger investor saving for retirement may

emphasize stocks and keep the bond allocation relatively modest, because the long runway allows more tolerance for volatility. An investor approaching retirement may increase the bond share to reduce sequence-of-returns risk and create a more stable pool of assets for near-term withdrawals. An investor concerned about inflation, geopolitical shocks, or commodity cycles may add a modest alternatives allocation to reduce dependence on the stock-bond relationship alone. The key is that each asset class should earn its place through a portfolio function, not through popularity or recent performance. A portfolio built around functions is easier to maintain than one built around headlines.

The interaction among stocks, bonds, and alternatives matters as much as the individual weights. A portfolio with 70 percent equities and 30 percent bonds can be riskier than it looks if the bond sleeve is concentrated in long-duration issues that are highly sensitive to rising rates. Likewise, adding an alternatives ETF does not automatically improve diversification if it is highly correlated with the rest of the portfolio during the periods that matter most. Asset allocation is therefore not just a math exercise in percentages; it is an exercise in understanding how the pieces behave together. Because passive vehicles now channel enormous capital flows and increasingly shape market structure, the composition of ETF-based allocations also has broader market significance [2]. For the individual investor, however, the practical question remains simpler: do the chosen sleeves complement one another in a way that supports the intended risk profile?

Implementation should also reflect the realities of account type and rebalancing. Taxable accounts may favor holdings with lower turnover and more tax-efficient distributions, while retirement accounts can be better suited to assets that generate more taxable income or require more frequent adjustment. Rebalancing is the mechanism that keeps the allocation from drifting too far from its target. If stocks rally sharply, the

equity sleeve can become too large and leave the portfolio more exposed than intended. If bonds or alternatives outperform, the portfolio may become more conservative than planned. The purpose of rebalancing is not to forecast the next winner. It is to restore the intended balance so that the portfolio continues to match the investor's risk budget over time.

A disciplined allocation across stocks, bonds, and alternatives also helps prevent a common mistake: confusing diversification with complexity. It is possible to own many ETFs and still have a portfolio that is overwhelmingly dependent on one economic outcome. It is also possible to hold only a few well-chosen funds and still achieve meaningful diversification if each one plays a distinct role. The asset allocation decision is where that discipline begins. Once the portfolio's major sleeves are defined, ETF selection becomes a matter of choosing efficient tools for each job, rather than searching for a fund that can somehow do every job at once.

Domestic versus international diversification

Domestic and international exposure serve different portfolio purposes, even when they are both delivered through broad market ETFs. Domestic funds usually anchor the portfolio in the investor's home economy, home currency, and home market institutions. That familiarity can be valuable because it reduces some of the uncertainty investors feel when they are evaluating businesses, earnings reports, and policy developments. It can also simplify tax reporting, trading, and portfolio monitoring. But familiarity is not the same as completeness. A portfolio that leans too heavily on the home market can leave an investor exposed to a narrow set of industries, a single monetary policy regime, and one country's economic cycle.

International diversification is useful because markets do not always move in lockstep. Different countries and regions can be at different

points in the business cycle, and their stock markets may be driven by different sector weights, valuation patterns, and policy responses. That means a portfolio with both domestic and foreign holdings may experience a smoother overall pattern of returns than one concentrated in a single market. Research on global allocations has also shown that investors often exhibit a strong home bias, holding more domestic assets than a purely risk-based framework would justify [25]. That bias is understandable, but it can limit the benefits diversification is supposed to provide.

The case for international ETFs is not simply that they add more holdings. It is that they add different sources of return and risk. A U.S. portfolio, for example, may be dominated by large technology and consumer-oriented firms, while a developed international fund may have greater exposure to financials, industrials, healthcare, or exporters tied to different demand patterns. Emerging market ETFs add another layer, often with higher growth potential but also greater volatility, currency sensitivity, and political risk. In portfolio terms, the question is not whether foreign markets are "better," but whether they improve the overall mix by reducing dependence on one country's outcomes.

Currency exposure is one of the main differences investors must understand. When an ETF holds foreign securities, its returns are affected not only by the local market performance of those securities but also by movements in the relevant currency relative to the investor's home currency. A foreign market can rise in local terms and still produce a weaker return for a U.S. investor if the foreign currency declines. The reverse is also true. This currency effect can either add diversification or introduce another source of volatility, depending on the fund and the market environment. Some ETFs hedge currency exposure, while others leave it unhedged, and that choice changes the role the fund plays in the portfolio.

There is also a difference between owning international equities for diversification and using them to make a specific macroeconomic bet. A broad developed-markets ETF is usually intended to capture the return characteristics of non-U.S. developed economies as a whole. A country-specific ETF, by contrast, is a more concentrated position and should be treated that way. The same is true for regional funds, frontier market funds, and sector-heavy foreign ETFs. An investor may think of all of them as "international," but their risk profiles can be very different. The more narrowly the fund is focused, the less it behaves like a diversification tool and the more it behaves like a targeted allocation.

The right balance between domestic and international exposure depends on the investor's goals, liabilities, and tolerance for unfamiliar risks. Investors who earn and spend in the same currency as their home market often want a substantial domestic core because it aligns assets with future obligations. At the same time, a meaningful international allocation can reduce concentration in one economy and one policy environment. That balance is especially important for long-term investors, because over decades the relative leadership of regions can change in ways that are difficult to predict. No single market stays on top forever, and diversification across countries is one way to avoid depending on that outcome.

ETF construction matters here as much as the geographic label. Two international funds can both appear broad, yet one may be weighted heavily toward a few large countries or industries while another spreads exposure more evenly across many markets. Some funds track market-capitalization indexes, which naturally assign more weight to the largest and most established foreign companies. Others use screens or alternative weighting methods that may tilt the portfolio away from the largest names. As with domestic ETFs, the index methodology determines what "international exposure" actually means in practice

[10]. Investors should therefore look beyond the fund's label and ask what part of the world, and what type of risk, the ETF is really delivering.

In many portfolios, the most durable approach is not to choose between domestic and international exposure, but to define how each should function. Domestic holdings can provide a stable foundation tied to the investor's home economy and currency. International holdings can broaden the opportunity set and reduce concentration. The key is to treat the split as a deliberate design choice rather than an afterthought. When that choice is made thoughtfully, geographic diversification becomes more than a slogan; it becomes a structural feature of the portfolio.

Rebalancing rules and portfolio maintenance

Rebalancing is the process of bringing a portfolio back toward its intended mix after market movements have pushed the weights away from target. If a portfolio starts at 60 percent equities and 40 percent bonds, it will not stay there for long. A strong stock market can lift the equity share well above target, while a bond rally or stock decline can pull it below. Left alone, the portfolio gradually becomes something different from the one the investor originally designed. Rebalancing is the discipline that keeps the portfolio aligned with its purpose, risk level, and expected behavior.

The first rule is to define the target allocation clearly enough that it can be measured. That means setting not only broad percentages for stocks, bonds, and other assets, but also deciding whether the portfolio will allow a range around each target. Many investors use bands rather than exact points because markets move continuously and constant adjustment creates unnecessary trading. A portfolio might be permitted to drift a few percentage points above or below its target before any action is taken. This approach recognizes that some variation is normal and that

the goal is not precision for its own sake, but control over the portfolio's overall risk profile.

Time-based rebalancing is the simplest method. Under this rule, the portfolio is reviewed on a fixed schedule, such as quarterly, semiannually, or annually, and adjustments are made if the weights have moved meaningfully away from target. The advantage is discipline: the investor does not have to make a judgment call every time markets fluctuate. The drawback is that a calendar alone may not reflect actual portfolio drift. A portfolio can become materially unbalanced long before the scheduled review, or it may require no changes at all when the date arrives. For that reason, many investors pair calendar reviews with tolerance bands so that the schedule becomes a checkpoint rather than the only trigger.

Threshold-based rebalancing focuses on the size of the drift rather than the passage of time. If an asset class moves beyond a preset band, the portfolio is adjusted back toward the target mix. This method can be more responsive to market conditions and can reduce the need for unnecessary trades when the portfolio remains close to plan. It also forces the investor to pay attention to concentration risk. When one part of the portfolio has appreciated sharply, the act of trimming it may feel uncomfortable, but that discomfort is often the point. Rebalancing can require selling what has done well and adding to what has lagged, which is contrary to instinct but consistent with risk control. Behavioral research has long shown that investors are vulnerable to emotional reactions such as overconfidence, recency bias, and the temptation to chase performance [99]. A rule-based rebalancing policy helps limit those impulses.

In practice, rebalancing does not always mean selling. New contributions, dividend reinvestment, and bond coupon flows can often be directed toward the underweight parts of the portfolio. That is usually

A practical maintenance routine usually includes three checks: whether the portfolio is still within its tolerance bands, whether any holdings have changed in quality or role, and whether the investor's own circumstances have changed enough to warrant a policy update. ETFs make this process easier because the building blocks are transparent and liquid, but that convenience should not encourage complacency. A portfolio that is never reviewed can drift far from its intended balance, while a portfolio that is adjusted too often can become expensive and unstable. The objective is to keep the portfolio intentional, not static.

position feel safer than it really is. Concentration risk becomes visible when the same forces that helped the sector rise begin to reverse. Earnings expectations can be reset, valuations can compress, and the ETF can decline even if the broader market remains stable. In that sense, sector exposure is a deliberate departure from market-wide diversification. It is a tactical or thematic choice, not a neutral building block.

Factor exposure risk is related but more subtle. A factor ETF may not be concentrated in a single industry, yet it can still lean heavily toward a shared style characteristic such as value, growth, momentum, quality, low volatility, or size. These factors are not free advantages; they are exposures with their own cycles. A portfolio tilted toward momentum may perform well when trends persist, but it can suffer when leadership changes abruptly. A low-volatility strategy may hold up better in some downturns, yet it can lag sharply in strong rallies. A value tilt can look attractive for long stretches and still underperform for years if the market continues to reward expensive growth companies. The risk is that an investor may believe a factor ETF is broadly diversified when, in practice, it is making a persistent bet on a particular return pattern.

These exposures often overlap with one another. A sector ETF may also carry a factor tilt, and a factor ETF may end up with meaningful sector concentration because the screening rules favor companies from the same industries. For example, a quality or momentum screen can cluster around a small set of large firms that satisfy the methodology, while a thematic ETF may combine both sector concentration and factor concentration in one product. That overlap matters because it can produce a portfolio that looks diversified by ticker count but is actually dependent on a limited set of economic conditions. The same problem appears when multiple ETFs are combined without checking their underlying composition. Two different funds may both appear to add variety while actually increasing exposure to the same sector, style, or set of market leaders.

Investors often underestimate this risk because ETF labels are convenient shorthand. A name that includes “innovation,” “growth,” “income,” or “low volatility” may suggest a broad and stable exposure, but the real question is what the index methodology selects and excludes. Index construction rules can create strong biases toward certain market capitalizations, industries, or balance-sheet characteristics. Research on index design and sustainability-oriented products has shown that the role of index providers is not passive in practice; the rules they set influence capital allocation and the exposures investors ultimately receive [21]. That same principle applies to sector and factor ETFs more generally. The methodology is not a technical footnote. It is the source of the risk profile.

Managing these risks begins with reading holdings, not just names. An investor should look at the top positions, the sector breakdown, and the factor characteristics if they are available. If one ETF places a large share of assets in a few names, or if several holdings are highly correlated, the fund may be more concentrated than expected. The same is true when a factor fund’s portfolio is dominated by one style regime. It is also useful to compare the ETF with the role it is supposed to play in the portfolio. A satellite position meant to express a view can tolerate concentration better than a core holding meant to anchor long-term returns. When the objective is broad market participation, a concentrated sector or factor fund should usually be treated as an addition, not a substitute, for diversified exposure.

The practical discipline is to measure how much of the portfolio depends on one story. That story may be the outlook for artificial intelligence, the path of oil prices, the shape of the yield curve, or the market’s preference for growth over value. If the answer is “a lot,” then the position is not merely an ETF choice; it is a conviction bet. Conviction bets can belong in a portfolio, but they should be sized with the understanding that concentration and factor tilts can dominate outcomes for long periods. In stress periods, those tilts can move together and amplify losses rather than offset them. The ETF structure makes these exposures easy to buy, but it does not make them less real.

Liquidity risk, volatility, and drawdown management

Liquidity risk in ETF investing is often misunderstood because investors tend to look only at the fund's average daily trading volume. That number matters, but it does not tell the whole story. A highly traded ETF can still become expensive to enter or exit if the underlying securities are thinly traded, if the market is under stress, or if trading occurs at an inconvenient time. In practice, liquidity has several layers: the liquidity of the ETF shares on the exchange, the liquidity of the securities inside the portfolio, and the liquidity of the market makers and authorized participants who help keep prices aligned. When those layers are healthy, an investor can usually trade efficiently. When they are strained, the cost of immediacy rises.

For this reason, a fund with modest share volume is not automatically illiquid in the way many beginners assume. Broad ETFs often remain tradable because the creation and redemption process gives large institutions a way to source shares even when the exchange volume is not extraordinary. The more relevant question is whether the underlying market can support efficient trading in the ETF's basket. A fund holding large-cap domestic stocks will usually be easier to trade than one holding small-cap equities, high-yield bonds, frontier markets, or less liquid alternatives. The ETF wrapper can improve access, but it does not erase the liquidity characteristics of the assets inside it.

Liquidity risk becomes more visible during periods of market stress. Bid-ask spreads can widen, premiums and discounts can grow, and execution quality can deteriorate even in products that usually trade smoothly. This is one reason why investors should avoid assuming that a fund's calm-day trading experience will persist under all conditions. In less liquid categories, the ETF may still provide an orderly market price, but that price can reflect a meaningful concession to urgency. The cost is not always obvious on the quote screen; it may appear as a larger spread, a less favorable fill, or a temporary disconnect between the ETF and the value of the underlying holdings.

Volatility is related but distinct. Liquidity risk is about how easily a position can be traded without moving the price against you; volatility is about how much the position's price moves in the first place. An ETF can be highly liquid and still very volatile if it tracks a narrow sector, a leveraged strategy, a single-country market, or a concentrated theme. Conversely, a less liquid bond ETF may show relatively modest day-to-day movement but still carry liquidity risk when investors try to trade in size. The distinction matters because investors sometimes mistake low trading volume for safety, when the real issue may be price instability, or mistake a calm chart for ease of exit, when the real issue may be market depth.

Drawdown management is the discipline of preparing for and responding to sustained declines rather than merely tolerating ordinary volatility. A drawdown is not just a bad day; it is a period in which the portfolio falls from a prior peak and may take time to recover. ETFs make drawdowns easier to observe because the portfolio is transparent and the price is continuously updated, but transparency does not soften the experience of loss. The best defense is to own exposures that match the investor's time horizon and risk tolerance, so that a decline does not force an emotional or financial liquidation at the wrong time. This is why position sizing, diversification, and rebalancing rules are not administrative details; they are part of drawdown control.

One practical way to manage drawdown risk is to ensure that no single ETF, sector, or style dominates the portfolio's outcome. A concentrated position can produce strong gains in favorable markets, but it can also create an outsized hole when conditions reverse. Holding a mix of assets with different return drivers can reduce the severity of portfolio-level declines, even if it does not eliminate them. For some investors, that means pairing equity ETFs with high-quality bond ETFs or cash equivalents. For others, it means limiting the size of thematic, sector, or factor tilts so that enthusiasm for a particular idea does not become a source of unnecessary fragility. Research on factor investing and specialized strategies consistently shows that the universe of return drivers is broad, but practical implementation requires restraint and attention to exposure overlap [66].

Behavior matters as much as construction. Investors often react to drawdowns by selling after losses have already accumulated, which locks in the decline and can make recovery harder. A more durable approach is to decide in advance how much volatility and drawdown a portfolio is allowed to experience and to build around that limit. That may include using limit orders when trading less liquid funds, avoiding the opening and closing minutes of the market when spreads can be wider, and rebalancing with a rules-based schedule rather than in response to headlines. It may also mean recognizing that an ETF with a compelling story, such as a narrow thematic or AI-related fund, can still produce very sharp swings because the underlying companies are often highly sensitive to sentiment and valuation changes [107]. The objective is not to eliminate risk, which is impossible, but to keep liquidity strain, volatility, and drawdown within a range that the investor can hold through without abandoning the plan.

Behavioral mistakes and how to stay disciplined

Behavioral mistakes often matter more than product selection because ETF portfolios are usually undermined by the investor, not the fund. The structure may be sound, the fees may be low, and the diversification may be adequate, yet poor timing and emotional reactions can still turn a reasonable plan into a disappointing result. This is one reason benchmark-oriented investing has become so important: once a portfolio is tied to a clear reference point, it becomes easier to see when decisions are driven by discipline and when they are driven by impulse [11].

One of the most common mistakes is performance chasing. Investors see a fund or a market segment that has recently outperformed and assume that recent winners will keep winning. In practice, that impulse tends to lead people to buy after enthusiasm has already been priced in and to sell after a drawdown has already created better long-term value. The problem is not only that the investor may be late; it is that the decision process becomes anchored to recent returns instead of to the role the ETF is supposed to play in the portfolio. A fund should be evaluated for its exposure, cost, and fit, not for whether it has been the most exciting holding over the last quarter.

Closely related is the habit of reacting to headlines. ETF investors can monitor markets constantly, and that convenience can create the illusion that every news item requires an immediate portfolio response. A geopolitical event, an inflation report, a central bank comment, or a sharp one-day decline can all feel urgent. But urgency is not the same as importance. Many headline-driven trades are simply attempts to reduce discomfort in the moment, and they often substitute short-term emotional relief for long-term portfolio discipline. Since passive vehicles now channel enormous amounts of capital through the market [2], these reactions can also become self-reinforcing when large groups of investors move together in the same direction.

Another behavioral error is confusing volatility with danger. A sharp price decline in an ETF can feel like evidence that the fund is broken, when it may simply reflect the normal risk of the underlying asset class. Investors who do not distinguish between temporary market movement and permanent impairment are more likely to abandon well-constructed positions at the wrong time. This is especially damaging when the ETF is part of a long-term allocation plan, because the investor may sell after a decline and then struggle to re-enter. Staying disciplined requires accepting in advance that discomfort is part of the price of exposure. If the portfolio is built to capture equity growth, credit income, or sector-specific upside, it will also occasionally endure periods when that exposure looks unattractive.

Overconfidence creates a different set of problems. Some investors believe that because ETFs are simple to trade, they are also simple to manage. That assumption can lead to excessive tinkering, frequent switching between similar funds, or repeated attempts to outguess the market with small tactical adjustments. A portfolio that is revised too often can accumulate trading costs, tax consequences, and decision fatigue without producing better outcomes. It can also become harder to evaluate, because the investor no longer knows whether performance is being driven by the market, the asset allocation, or a series of reactive choices. Discipline is easier to maintain when each trade has a clear purpose and a defined place in the overall plan.

There is also a tendency to overestimate what diversification means. Holding several ETFs does not automatically create resilience if the funds overlap heavily or respond to the same economic forces. An investor may own multiple products and still be concentrated in the same large-cap growth names, the same duration risk, or the same sector exposure. When that happens, the portfolio may feel diversified because it contains many tickers, but it behaves like a much narrower bet. This can encourage the false conclusion that the strategy failed when, in reality, the strategy was never truly diversified in the first place. Clear allocation rules help prevent this by forcing the investor to ask what each fund contributes that the others do not.

Staying disciplined is partly a matter of process. A written investment policy, even a simple one, can reduce impulsive behavior by defining target allocations, rebalancing ranges, and the conditions under which a position may be changed. That kind of structure matters because it shifts the investor's attention from feelings to rules. It also helps to separate research from execution: a fund can be evaluated during calm periods, while trades can be made only after the decision has survived a cooling-off period. For many investors, automation is another useful safeguard. Automatic contributions and scheduled rebalancing reduce the number of moments in which emotion can interfere with judgment.

Discipline also depends on how expectations are framed. If an investor expects every ETF to outperform at all times, disappointment is inevitable. A broad market fund will not always lead the market, a bond ETF will not always protect capital in a rising-rate environment, and a thematic ETF may lag for long stretches before any potential thesis plays out. The goal is not to eliminate uncertainty but to endure it without abandoning a sound plan. That is easier when each holding has a defined purpose, the portfolio is sized appropriately, and the investor understands that a good process can still produce uneven short-term results. In that sense, discipline is less about emotional control in the abstract than about designing a portfolio that makes emotional control easier to practice.

CHAPTER 8

Chapter 8: Advanced ETF Strategies and Use Cases

Once an ETF portfolio is in place, the question often shifts from construction to implementation: how to adjust exposures without abandoning discipline or turning a long-term plan into a series of reactive trades. That is where advanced uses of ETFs come into view. The same structure that makes ETFs efficient and transparent for core investing can also make them useful for managing transitions, expressing measured views, and handling periods when capital needs to remain available but not idle. Used well, these applications are less about prediction than about control—controlling timing, controlling tax consequences, and controlling the way portfolio changes are introduced.

Tactical asset allocation and portfolio tilts

Tactical asset allocation uses ETFs to make deliberate, usually temporary adjustments to a strategic portfolio. The strategic allocation is the long-term design: the mix of stocks, bonds, and other exposures that reflects the investor's objectives and risk tolerance. Tactical allocation sits on top of that structure and asks a narrower question: given current conditions, should the portfolio lean a little more toward one area and a little less toward another? In ETF form, this can be implemented quickly and transparently, which is one reason ETFs have become a practical tool for investors who want to express a view without rebuilding the entire portfolio.

The key distinction is that a tactical move is not meant to replace the strategic plan. It is a tilt, not a new foundation. An investor with a balanced long-term allocation may choose to add a modest overweight to short-duration bonds when interest-rate sensitivity appears unattractive, or to trim a broad market equity position in favor of a more defensive equity segment when volatility rises. The point is to adjust exposure in measured increments rather than to make large, all-or-nothing bets. That restraint matters because the more a tactical position dominates the portfolio, the more the portfolio begins to behave like a forecast instead of a plan.

ETF tilts can be built around several dimensions. An investor may tilt by asset class, such as moving slightly above target in equities and below target in cash or bonds when risk appetite is strong. The tilt may also be regional, favoring domestic over international exposure or vice versa. It may be style-based, shifting toward value, quality, low volatility, or momentum depending on the investor's views about the market environment. Sector tilts are also common, though they carry greater concentration risk because they depend on narrow parts of the economy. Factor-based tilts deserve particular caution: the academic literature has identified a very large number of candidate factors, but only a subset are robust enough to be useful in practice, and practical implementation requires discipline, diversification, and a clear rationale [66].

The attraction of ETFs in this setting is that they make the implementation clean. A portfolio manager does not need to buy dozens of individual securities to express a view about a segment of the market. A single ETF can shift the portfolio toward a desired exposure, and the position can later be reduced or closed with relatively little operational complexity. That simplicity is especially useful when the goal is to make a small tactical adjustment around a core portfolio rather than to redesign the core itself. It is also useful when the investor wants to separate the strategic allocation from a shorter-term overlay, a distinction that has long been emphasized in benchmark-oriented portfolio management [11] [92].

Even so, tactical allocation should be governed by rules, not impulse. A tilt should have a reason, a size limit, and an exit condition. Without those three elements, it becomes difficult to tell whether the position is a disciplined expression of a view or simply a reaction to recent market movement. Investors often make the mistake of treating recent performance as evidence that a theme will continue, when in fact the market may already have priced in much of the story. A tactical ETF position should therefore be tied to a specific thesis, such as relative valuation, earnings breadth, interest-rate expectations, or risk reduction, and the thesis should be reviewed against observable evidence rather than headlines.

Portfolio tilts also need to be evaluated in the context of the whole portfolio, not just the ETF itself. A defensive equity ETF may look conservative on its own, but if the rest of the portfolio is already concentrated in similar exposures, the tilt may not add much diversification benefit. Likewise, a commodity ETF may seem attractive as a short-term inflation hedge, but commodity exposure has its own distinct behavior and can be difficult to fit into a portfolio if the investor does not understand its role and limitations [49]. The same is true for alternative or skill-based strategies: they may provide different return drivers, but they are not substitutes for a coherent asset allocation framework [16].

Costs and trading behavior matter more in tactical strategies than they do in static buy-and-hold positions because tactical investors trade more often. The expense ratio still matters, but so do bid-ask spreads, market impact, and the possibility that a short-lived tilt is undone by implementation friction. A tactical ETF that is cheap on paper can become expensive if it is traded repeatedly in thin conditions or if the investor enters and exits at poor times. For that reason, tactical allocation works best when the position size is modest, the holding period is purposeful, and the trade is large enough to matter but not so large that it distorts the long-term plan.

Portfolio tilts are most effective when they are treated as structured deviations from a benchmark rather than as a substitute for one. The benchmark provides the reference point, the strategic allocation provides the anchor, and the tilt defines the temporary deviation. That framework helps investors avoid a common error: confusing conviction with concentration. A well-designed tactical ETF position should be understandable, limited, and reversible. It should add value only if the investor's view proves correct, and it should not jeopardize the broader portfolio if that view does not.

Using ETFs for tax efficiency and portfolio transitions

Using ETFs for tax efficiency often comes down to understanding when a portfolio change can be made inside the fund structure rather than by selling one position and buying another in the open market. In a taxable account, that distinction matters. A traditional sale of appreciated securities can trigger a realized capital gain, while an ETF can sometimes adjust its holdings through in-kind creation and redemption activity that does not require the fund to sell appreciated positions in the same way a mutual fund might. The result is not that ETFs are "tax-free," but that their structure can help defer taxable gains and reduce the frequency of distributions. That structural advantage has been one reason passive and exchange-traded vehicles have become so widely used in taxable investing [48][53].

The tax benefit is strongest when the ETF is used as a long-term holding and the investor is not forcing unnecessary turnover at the portfolio level. A low-turnover broad market ETF can be especially efficient because the fund itself is not constantly realizing gains, and the investor can often avoid realizing gains until a personal decision to sell. This creates a useful separation between market exposure and taxable realization. Even when the fund does distribute dividends or interest, the investor still preserves control over the timing of capital gains realization, which can be valuable for households managing annual income brackets, harvesting losses, or coordinating sales with other taxable events. In this sense, ETF tax efficiency is partly a matter of product design and partly a matter of investor discipline.

The same logic becomes especially useful during portfolio transitions. Investors rarely move from one allocation to another in a single step. They may be shifting from a concentrated stock position into a diversified portfolio, moving from a growth-oriented mix toward more income-oriented exposures, or replacing a legacy mutual fund lineup with a more streamlined ETF structure. If those changes are made by selling every old holding at once, the tax bill can become a major obstacle. ETFs can help because they allow the transition to be staged. An investor can build the desired new allocation gradually, direct new contributions into the target ETFs, and then sell legacy positions in tax-aware increments rather than all at once. This reduces the chance that the portfolio change itself becomes more costly than the investment improvement it was meant to produce.

In some cases, an ETF is not just the destination but the bridge. Suppose an investor wants to move from a concentrated employer stock position into a diversified equity allocation. Selling the stock immediately may create a large taxable gain. Instead, the investor may use a broad ETF as the receiving vehicle while trimming the concentrated position over time, pairing sales with loss harvesting elsewhere in the portfolio or with years when taxable income is lower. The ETF gives the investor a liquid, diversified landing point while the transition unfolds. The same approach can be used when reorienting a portfolio after retirement, after the sale of a business, or after a major change in risk tolerance. The key advantage is flexibility: the ETF can absorb capital efficiently while the investor manages the tax consequences of leaving an old position.

Tax-loss harvesting is another area where ETFs are often used with precision. When a holding has declined below its cost basis, an investor may sell it to realize the loss and use a similar but not identical ETF to maintain market exposure. This preserves the portfolio's strategic allocation while capturing a tax loss that may offset gains elsewhere. The technique is straightforward in concept but requires care in execution. The replacement ETF should be sufficiently similar to keep the portfolio's risk profile intact, but not so similar that it creates problems under the wash sale rules. Because ETFs are available in many overlapping forms—broad market, large-cap, value, growth, sector, and regional—the investor often has room to make a controlled substitution without abandoning the intended exposure.

Portfolio transitions also benefit from the way ETFs can be combined with cash management. If a portfolio is being restructured over several months, an investor does not need to leave proceeds idle in a checking account or rush into a final allocation before the plan is ready. Short-duration bond ETFs, Treasury ETFs, and other cash-equivalent exposures can serve as temporary parking places while the transition is completed. That can reduce the temptation to keep cash uninvested for too long, while still allowing a measured sequence of trades. The transition itself becomes part of the portfolio process rather than a disruptive event.

The tax efficiency of ETFs should still be viewed in context. Not every ETF is equally efficient, and not every account benefits equally from the same strategy. High-yield bond ETFs, commodity ETFs, or actively managed funds may generate more taxable income or more frequent distributions than a broad equity index ETF. In retirement accounts, where current taxation is deferred, the relative advantage of ETF tax efficiency may be less important than in a taxable brokerage account. But when the account is taxable, and especially when the investor is making a major allocation shift, ETFs can provide a practical way to control realization, manage timing, and move from one portfolio structure to another without letting taxes dictate the entire process.

Hedging, cash management, and temporary parking strategies

ETFs can be useful when an investor wants exposure without committing all available capital at once, but the role they play in that setting should be defined clearly. Hedging is not the same as return seeking. A hedge is a position intended to offset a specific risk in another holding or in a broader portfolio. In ETF form, that can mean using an index fund, a bond fund, a currency-sensitive fund, or a sector-specific fund to reduce the impact of a known vulnerability. The key is precision: the ETF should be chosen for its relationship to the risk being managed, not because it appears defensive in a general sense. A broad market ETF may soften idiosyncratic risk if it replaces a concentrated stock position, but it will not protect against a market-wide decline. Likewise, a bond ETF may help offset equity volatility, yet its effectiveness depends on duration, credit quality, and the interest rate environment.

Because ETFs are transparent and tradable, they are often used to implement hedges more efficiently than by trading individual securities. An investor with a large equity portfolio may use a short-term Treasury ETF or a broad bond ETF to reduce overall portfolio volatility, especially when the concern is temporary rather than strategic. A portfolio exposed to foreign assets may use a currency-hedged ETF if the goal is to isolate equity or bond returns from exchange-rate movements. A concentrated sector position can sometimes be offset with a broad market or inverse-like exposure, though the hedge may be imperfect if the concentrated holding behaves differently from the index used to offset it. The point is not to make risk disappear; it is to reshape the portfolio so that one source of loss is less likely to dominate the whole account.

Temporary parking strategies sit closer to cash management than to hedging, but the two often overlap in practice. When money is waiting for deployment—after a sale, before a purchase, or during a phased entry plan—an investor may want the funds to remain accessible while avoiding the drag of sitting entirely in cash. Cash-equivalent ETFs and very short-duration bond ETFs are commonly used for this purpose because they provide a modest yield and daily liquidity while generally carrying less price volatility than longer-duration fixed-income funds. That said, "temporary" does not mean risk-free. Even short-duration bond ETFs can fluctuate when rates move, and funds tied to commercial paper, floating-rate instruments, or ultra-short credit exposure may respond differently under stress. The investor should understand whether the fund is meant to preserve nominal value, maintain liquidity, or simply reduce the opportunity cost of waiting.

The useful comparison is not between an ETF and cash in the abstract, but between the ETF and the specific cash need. If the money is needed on a known date in the near future, an investor may prefer the simplest possible vehicle that minimizes uncertainty. If the funds may remain idle for months, an ETF can serve as a more efficient parking place than a non-interest-bearing account, provided the investor accepts that the market value can still move. This is particularly relevant in portfolio transitions, where proceeds from one position are being held before reinvestment. In that setting, the objective is usually to avoid taking unnecessary market risk while also avoiding the complete forfeiture of yield. An ETF can be a middle ground, but only if its duration, credit exposure, and trading characteristics fit the time frame involved.

One practical issue in both hedging and parking strategies is that the ETF's structure can create mismatches between what the investor expects and what the fund actually delivers. A bond ETF that appears conservative may still lose value if interest rates rise sharply. A commodity ETF may hedge inflation in one period and fail to do so in another because the relevant commodity does not move in lockstep with consumer prices. A cash-like ETF may hold short-dated instruments that look stable most of the time but can still experience spread widening or price pressure when markets become strained. Investors should therefore think in terms of correlation and duration, not just labels such as "safe," "defensive," or "cash alternative." The more closely the intended hedge or parking role is tied to a measurable risk, the easier it is to judge whether the ETF is doing its job.

Cost and execution matter as well, especially when the position is meant to be temporary. A strategy designed to hold capital for only a short period can be undermined by spreads, commissions, or poor trade timing if the investor enters and exits carelessly. In a parking position, the yield advantage over cash may be modest, so a wide bid-ask spread can consume a meaningful share of the benefit. In a hedge, the investor may need to rebalance more than once as conditions change, which means trading friction can accumulate. For that reason, highly liquid

ETFs are often preferred for short-term uses, not because they are inherently safer, but because they are easier to move in and out of with less price impact. This is one area where the operational details of ETF trading become part of the risk-management decision itself.

Disciplined use of these strategies also requires restraint. Investors sometimes turn temporary parking into a permanent holding pattern, waiting for a perfect entry point that never arrives, or they may use a hedge so aggressively that the portfolio no longer reflects the returns they actually need. A hedge should be sized to the risk it is meant to offset, and a parking position should be tied to a real time horizon rather than to vague discomfort with volatility. In both cases, the ETF is a tool for managing uncertainty, not a substitute for making the underlying allocation decision. Used that way, it can help preserve flexibility, reduce avoidable exposure, and keep capital working while the investor waits for the next deliberate step.

Incorporating thematic and factor ETFs with discipline

Thematic and factor ETFs can be useful tools, but they work best when they are treated as deliberate portfolio instruments rather than as expressions of excitement about a story. A thematic ETF is usually built around a narrative such as clean energy, artificial intelligence, cybersecurity, or aging demographics. A factor ETF, by contrast, is designed around a persistent characteristic that the sponsor believes can explain return behavior, such as value, momentum, quality, low volatility, or size. In both cases, the appeal is that the investor can access a targeted idea in a single trade instead of assembling it security by security. The risk is that the same focus that makes these funds interesting can also make them unstable, crowded, or difficult to hold through a full market cycle.

The first discipline is to ask what problem the fund is actually solving. A thematic ETF may be appropriate when an investor wants a narrow expression of conviction without making a concentrated single-stock bet. A factor ETF may be appropriate when the goal is to tilt a portfolio toward a style that has a long record of use in institutional investing. But neither type should be added simply because it sounds modern or because recent performance has been strong. Research on retail investor behavior shows that access, convenience, and simplified product design can encourage more frequent trading and more reactive decision-making, especially when platforms make purchase decisions feel effortless [119]. That matters here because thematic and factor ETFs often arrive with a persuasive narrative that can disguise the fact that the position is still subject to ordinary market risk.

It is also important to separate a theme from a business cycle story. Some themes are tied to structural change, while others are little more than a current market favorite packaged into a fund. A theme may have genuine long-term relevance and still be a poor investment if the underlying companies are expensive, unprofitable, or heavily dependent on future capital raising. Thematic ETFs can also overlap heavily with broad market holdings, which means they may not add as much diversification as investors assume. In effect, the fund can become a concentrated bet on a small group of names that are already widely owned elsewhere in the portfolio. That is why the holdings list matters more than the label on the prospectus. If a thematic ETF owns only a handful of dominant stocks, the investor should think of it as a satellite position, not a second core.

Factor ETFs deserve the same scrutiny, even though they are often presented in more technical language. A factor strategy is not a guarantee of superior returns; it is a way of organizing exposure to a particular pattern in the market. Value, momentum, quality, and low-volatility funds can each behave differently depending on the market regime, and each can lag for extended periods. That lag is not necessarily a sign that the fund is broken. It may simply mean the factor is out of favor. The discipline required here is patience and position sizing. A factor tilt should be modest enough that an investor can tolerate a long stretch of underperformance without abandoning the strategy at the wrong time. Otherwise, the fund may be purchased at the peak of enthusiasm and sold after disappointment has already set in.

Selection discipline also means examining how the theme or factor is implemented. Two funds can use the same broad label and still deliver meaningfully different exposures. One clean energy ETF may hold manufacturers, utilities, and equipment suppliers, while another concentrates in a smaller set of developers and technology enablers. One quality factor ETF may screen for profitability and balance-sheet strength, while another may emphasize earnings stability or return on equity. The index methodology determines whether the fund is truly aligned with the investor's intent or simply borrowing a familiar marketing term. Sustainable and ESG-branded funds provide a useful reminder of this point: research has shown that self-labeled ESG funds do not always hold the stakeholder-friendly companies investors may expect [24], and the broader literature on sustainable ETFs continues to emphasize variation in design and screening approach [40]. The lesson is not that these funds are unusable, but that labels should never replace inspection.

Cost and turnover deserve special attention as well. Thematic and factor ETFs often charge more than plain vanilla market funds, and higher fees need to be justified by a clear role in the portfolio. They may also rebalance more frequently than broad index funds, which can increase trading costs and create more volatility in the holdings mix. For taxable investors, frequent turnover can also reduce after-tax efficiency.

A disciplined investor therefore compares the fund's expense ratio, its turnover history, and its actual holdings drift against the intended purpose of the position. If the fund is expensive, narrow, and difficult to explain in portfolio terms, it should probably be small or omitted entirely.

The most effective way to use these ETFs is to limit them to a defined role and a defined size. They work best as satellites around a diversified core, with clear rules for entry, review, and exit. That means deciding in advance whether the position is meant to express a long-term structural view, a measured style tilt, or a temporary allocation decision. It also means resisting the urge to reclassify a disappointed theme as a "long-term opportunity" every time it falls behind. Discipline is not only about buying carefully; it is about preserving the difference between a purposeful allocation and a speculative impulse dressed in fund form.

CHAPTER 9

Chapter 9: Taxes, Fees, and the Real Cost of ETF Investing

Once an investor moves from comparing ETFs in the abstract to actually owning them, the discussion naturally shifts from product features to the economic drag that can shape results over time. A fund's published fee is only one part of that picture, and it can be misleading to treat it as the whole story. The real cost of ETF investing also depends on how the fund trades, how it behaves in different account types, and whether its structure creates tax consequences that are easy to overlook when the position is first purchased.

Expense ratios versus trading costs and spreads

The expense ratio is the most visible cost in an ETF, but it is not the only cost that matters, and it is often not the largest cost an investor experiences in practice. The expense ratio is deducted from fund assets over time, so it acts as a persistent drag on performance rather than a one-time charge. Trading costs and bid-ask spreads, by contrast, show up when shares are bought or sold, and they depend on how the market is behaving at the moment of execution. A low expense ratio can therefore be misleading if the ETF is expensive to trade, especially for investors who enter and exit positions frequently or who place orders in less favorable market conditions.

This distinction matters because the cost of owning an ETF is partly visible and partly embedded. The expense ratio is published and easy to compare, which is one reason investors focus on it so heavily. But the actual implementation cost can also include the spread between the bid and ask price, market impact from larger orders, commissions if a broker still charges them, and the opportunity cost of poor execution. For investors who trade rarely and hold for long periods, the expense ratio will usually be the dominant cost. For active traders, tactical allocators, and investors using specialized or thinly traded funds, trading frictions can matter just as much as the annual fee.

Bid-ask spreads are especially important because they represent the immediate price paid to get into or out of a position. In a highly liquid ETF, that spread may be very small, but in a narrower fund it can widen enough to offset years of fee savings. A fund with a very low expense ratio can still be a poor choice if the spread is consistently wide or if the underlying securities are difficult to trade. This is one reason ETF quality cannot be judged by cost alone. The structure of the portfolio, the liquidity of the holdings, and the level of market participation all influence how cheaply the shares can be transacted. Research on ETF performance has repeatedly shown that tracking outcomes and realized investor returns depend on more than the headline fee, because implementation frictions can alter the return an investor actually experiences [97].

The difference between expense ratio and trading cost also becomes clearer when the investment horizon changes. Over a long holding period, a small difference in annual fees compounds steadily, so a lower expense ratio can be meaningful even if the ETF is traded only once. By contrast, a spread is paid each time shares are bought or sold, so repeated trading can make a low-cost ETF surprisingly expensive to use. This is why some funds that look inexpensive on paper are not necessarily the cheapest in practice. An investor who trades a fund once and holds it for years may care most about the published fee, while an investor who rebalances often may care more about spread width, execution quality, and how the fund behaves around the open and close of the market.

It is also useful to distinguish between the cost of accessing an ETF and the cost of maintaining it. The expense ratio reflects the fund sponsor's ongoing charge for managing the portfolio, operating the fund, and providing the structure that keeps it functioning. Trading costs are transactional and depend on the investor's behavior as much as on the fund itself. That means two investors can own the same ETF and pay very different total costs. One may buy patiently during liquid market hours, use limit orders, and hold for years. Another may trade frequently, use market orders in volatile sessions, and incur spreads and slippage that dwarf the fund's annual fee. The ETF has not changed, but the realized cost has.

Investors should also be careful not to treat "cheap" as synonymous with "efficient." A very low expense ratio is attractive, but it does not guarantee that the fund is easy to trade, well constructed, or suitable for the intended role in a portfolio. The broader literature on passive investing and fund design has emphasized that low cost is a central advantage of index-based vehicles, but it is only one dimension of fund selection [53]. In practice, the cheapest fund on a fee schedule may not be the cheapest fund to own once spreads, turnover, and execution are considered. This is especially true in less liquid segments of the market, where the underlying securities themselves may be harder to price and trade.

For that reason, the most useful comparison is not expense ratio versus trading cost as competing ideas, but expense ratio plus trading cost as components of total ownership cost. The fee is the background drag; the spread and execution costs are the front-end and back-end friction. A disciplined investor evaluates both. That usually means comparing funds with similar exposures, checking whether the trading spread is consistently narrow, and considering how often the position will be adjusted. It also means recognizing that the right answer may differ by account type and by strategy. A long-term core holding can justify more attention to annual fees, while a tactical sleeve or a short-term allocation may require much more attention to how cheaply the position can actually be entered and exited.

Capital gains distributions and tax efficiency

Capital gains distributions are one of the main ways an ETF can create an unexpected tax bill in a taxable account, even when the investor never sells a share. A distribution occurs when the fund realizes gains inside the portfolio and passes them through to shareholders. Those gains are usually classified as short term or long term depending on how long the fund held the underlying position before selling it, and that classification affects how they are taxed. The important point is that the tax event belongs to the shareholder, not just the fund. An ETF can be a highly tax-efficient vehicle overall and still distribute gains in a given year if its portfolio changes in a way that forces realized profits to be passed along.

The likelihood of distributions depends heavily on how the ETF is managed and what it holds. Broad, index-based stock ETFs often have relatively low turnover and can use in-kind creation and redemption activity to help manage embedded gains inside the fund structure. That is one reason passive investing has become so attractive to many investors: it combines diversification with lower ongoing costs and, in many cases, more favorable tax behavior than higher-turnover strategies [53]. By contrast, ETFs that rebalance frequently, follow narrow or fast-changing indexes, or hold less liquid securities may be more likely to realize gains. Sector funds, thematic funds, and actively managed ETFs can all be efficient tools, but they may generate more taxable distributions than a broad market fund simply because their portfolios change more often.

The structure of the ETF matters because it can reduce, though not eliminate, the need to sell appreciated holdings in the open market. In-kind transfers allow the fund to exchange securities rather than liquidate them, which can help the ETF avoid passing realized gains through to shareholders. This mechanism is a major reason ETFs are often described as tax efficient. But investors should not confuse "tax efficient" with "tax free." If the fund must sell securities to meet redemptions, adjust its strategy, or respond to index changes, gains can still be realized. Funds that operate in less liquid markets, or that must rebalance around concentrated exposures, may have fewer opportunities to use the most tax-friendly mechanisms.

Tax efficiency also depends on what kind of return the fund is generating. A fund can distribute ordinary income, interest, qualified dividends, or capital gains, and each category is treated differently in a taxable account. Bond ETFs, for example, may be efficient in trading terms but still produce regular taxable income because the underlying coupon payments are passed through to shareholders. Equity ETFs may be more likely to benefit from favorable capital gains treatment, yet even there the mix of distributions can vary materially from fund to fund. Investors who focus only on yield can miss the fact that a high distribution rate may simply reflect taxable income being paid out, not necessarily a superior after-tax result.

The timing of distributions is another reason investors need to pay attention. An ETF can trade at a seemingly attractive price shortly before a distribution, only for the buyer to receive a taxable payment that was effectively embedded in the purchase price. This is why the record date, ex-dividend date, and distribution estimate matter in taxable accounts. A fund with a low expense ratio may still be a poor after-tax choice if it regularly distributes gains at inconvenient times. The reverse is also true: a slightly more expensive fund can sometimes be the better holding if its structure keeps taxable distributions low over long periods. Research on fund regulation and taxation has long shown that the legal and structural design of pooled vehicles can materially affect investor outcomes [48].

For investors managing taxable accounts, the practical task is to look beyond the headline description of an ETF and ask how it behaves in real tax terms. That means checking distribution history, turnover, index methodology, and whether the fund has a pattern of realizing gains after reconstitutions or portfolio shifts. It also means recognizing that not all "green," thematic, or specialty strategies behave the same way. Funds tied to emerging policy themes or concentrated sectors may experience more pronounced volatility and portfolio turnover, which can influence both returns and taxable distributions. Studies of specialized ETF segments, including energy and green-related funds, show that these products can differ meaningfully in return behavior and spillover characteristics [20][28]. The broader lesson is that tax efficiency is not a label attached to the ETF wrapper itself; it is an outcome produced by the fund's holdings, trading behavior, and portfolio management process.

In retirement accounts, the issue is simpler because current taxation is deferred or sheltered, so capital gains distributions are less immediately relevant to the investor's annual tax bill. In taxable accounts, however, they can change the effective return of an ETF in a way that is easy to overlook when comparing funds side by side. A disciplined comparison therefore looks at both pre-tax performance and the likely after-tax experience. That is especially important for investors who use ETFs as long-term core holdings, because a fund that appears efficient on paper can still create avoidable tax friction if its distribution profile is poorly matched to the account in which it is held.

Taxable accounts versus retirement accounts

The account type matters because the same ETF can produce very different after-tax results depending on where it is held. In a taxable account, dividends, interest, and realized capital gains can all create current tax consequences. In a retirement account, those same cash flows are generally sheltered while assets remain inside the account, which changes how much attention an investor needs to pay to distribution timing, turnover, and tax efficiency. The distinction is not about whether the ETF is "good" or "bad"; it is about whether the account will absorb the fund's tax characteristics or pass them through to the investor.

Taxable accounts tend to reward ETFs that are efficient at limiting distributions and managing turnover. A broad equity ETF with low turnover may be especially attractive here because it often generates fewer taxable events than an actively traded strategy. That does not mean taxable investors should avoid all higher-turnover funds, but it does mean they should understand that frequent trading inside the portfolio can create realized gains that become taxable even if the investor never sells. For long-term investors, this is one reason index-based equity ETFs have become so widely used in taxable portfolios: they can offer diversified exposure while helping reduce the annual tax drag associated with portfolio churn.

Retirement accounts change the analysis. Because taxes are typically deferred until money is withdrawn, the investor is less concerned with annual distributions and more concerned with the fund's role in the portfolio. That makes retirement accounts a natural home for ETFs that might be less tax-efficient in a taxable setting, such as certain bond ETFs, higher-turnover strategies, or funds that regularly distribute income. The absence of immediate taxation does not eliminate all cost differences, but it does reduce the importance of distribution management as a day-to-day selection criterion. In that environment, the investor can focus more directly on risk, return, and portfolio fit.

Bond ETFs illustrate the difference clearly. Interest from bonds is usually taxed as ordinary income in taxable accounts, which can make fixed-income exposure relatively expensive to hold outside a tax-advantaged wrapper. The tax burden can be especially noticeable for investors in higher brackets or for those using bond funds as a substantial part of their allocation. Inside a retirement account, however, the same bond ETF can serve its stabilizing role without producing an annual tax bill. That is why many investors prefer to place tax-inefficient fixed income in retirement accounts when they have the flexibility to do so.

Equity ETFs can also be affected by account placement, though often in subtler ways. A broad market ETF may distribute modest dividends, while a dividend-focused ETF may distribute more income and therefore create more taxable cash flow. International ETFs can add another layer of complexity because foreign withholding taxes may apply in some cases, and the investor may or may not be able to use a foreign tax credit depending on the account type and the specific fund structure. These details do not automatically make one account type superior, but they do make it important to match the ETF's tax profile with the account's purpose.

Account location becomes especially important when an investor is building a portfolio across multiple accounts. The question is not only which ETFs to own, but where to place each one. A common approach is to reserve taxable accounts for holdings that are relatively tax-efficient and to use retirement accounts for positions that are more likely to distribute taxable income or realize gains internally. This is a form of asset location, and it can improve after-tax results without changing the overall strategic allocation. It also helps preserve flexibility: the investor can hold the same general mix of stocks and bonds while arranging them in the most tax-aware way available.

At the same time, taxes should not override every other consideration. A slightly less tax-efficient ETF may still be the best choice if it offers better diversification, lower implementation risk, or a more appropriate exposure for the portfolio. Account placement should support the investment plan, not distort it. For example, a retiree drawing from a retirement account may care more about income stability and risk control than about annual tax efficiency inside that account, while a younger investor with a large taxable brokerage account may place much greater emphasis on minimizing distributions and turnover. The right answer depends on the investor's tax bracket, time horizon, account mix, and withdrawal plans, not on any single rule applied mechanically.

How to compare ETF costs in real-world terms

The first step in comparing ETF costs in real-world terms is to move beyond the published expense ratio and ask what actually leaves the investor's pocket over the life of the position. The expense ratio is still important, but it is only one layer of cost. A fund with a very low published fee can still be expensive to own if it trades with wide spreads, sits in a thin market, or creates tax consequences that are easy to overlook. Conversely, a fund with a slightly higher expense ratio may be the cheaper choice overall if it is highly liquid, tracks efficiently, and is easier to trade in size. The point is not to ignore the fee schedule; it is to place it inside the full economic picture.

A useful way to think about ETF cost is to separate it into recurring costs and transaction costs. Recurring costs include the expense ratio and, in some cases, the drag from portfolio turnover or securities lending practices that affect the fund's net return. Transaction costs include the bid-ask spread, commissions if they still apply at a given brokerage, and the market impact of entering or exiting the position at an inconvenient time. For a long-term investor who buys once and holds for years, the expense ratio may dominate. For an investor who trades more often, or uses smaller position sizes, the spread can matter just as much as the annual fee because it is paid every time the position changes.

Real-world cost comparison also requires a time horizon. A difference of 5 basis points per year may look trivial in isolation, but over a decade or more it compounds. On the other hand, a one-time spread cost of 10 or 20 basis points can be less important if the fund is held for a long period and the expense ratio is meaningfully lower than alternatives. This is why a strict focus on the lowest published fee can be misleading. The cheapest ETF on paper is not always the cheapest ETF in practice, especially if the investor must pay more to get in and out of it or if the fund's structure causes the return to fall short of what the benchmark suggests.

The comparison becomes more concrete when the investor estimates the dollar cost of a position rather than only the percentage cost. Suppose two ETFs both provide similar exposure. One charges 0.03 percent annually and trades with a very tight spread; the other charges 0.10 percent annually and has a wider spread. If the position is small and the investor trades infrequently, the annual fee difference may amount to only a few dollars per year, while the spread difference may be the larger concern at the moment of purchase. If the position is large and held for many years, the annual fee difference may eventually overtake the initial trading friction. Thinking in dollars makes those tradeoffs easier to see because it turns abstract basis points into a cost that can be compared with expected portfolio benefit.

It also helps to distinguish between costs that are visible and costs that are embedded. The expense ratio is visible because it is disclosed directly. Spread costs are less obvious because they are reflected in the price the investor receives rather than in a separate line item. Tax costs can be even less visible because they may not appear until year-end or until the position is sold. In a taxable account, an ETF that regularly distributes capital gains can create a larger after-tax burden than a slightly more expensive fund that is more tax efficient. Passive investors now control a very large share of market assets, which makes tax treatment, trading behavior, and fund structure increasingly important in portfolio outcomes [2]. That is one reason cost comparison should include the account type, not just the fund label.

The comparison also changes depending on how the ETF is being used. For a core holding in a retirement account, the investor may reasonably place heavier weight on the expense ratio and tracking quality, since taxes are deferred and trading may be infrequent. For a tactical position, a sector tilt, or a short-term allocation, liquidity and spread can become the dominant costs because the position may be entered and exited more often. In those cases, the cheapest fund by fee may be the more expensive fund to use if it is difficult to trade efficiently. Liquidity is not just a convenience feature; it is part of the cost structure that affects the actual price of implementation [6].

A disciplined comparison therefore asks a few practical questions. How much will it cost to buy the ETF today, including spread and any commissions? How much will it cost to hold it for the intended period, including the expense ratio and any expected tracking drag? How much tax friction might it create in the account where it is held? And if the fund is sold later, how liquid is the market likely to be under normal and stressed conditions? Those questions turn ETF selection into a total-cost decision rather than a fee-shopping exercise. In that frame, the investor is not simply asking which fund is cheapest, but which fund delivers the desired exposure at the lowest all-in cost for the way it will actually be used.

CHAPTER 10

Chapter 10: Common Mistakes and How to Avoid Them

Even a well-constructed ETF portfolio can be weakened by decisions made after the purchase, and those decisions are often driven less by analysis than by impatience, simplification, or a misplaced sense that all funds with the same label must behave alike. The most common errors are not usually dramatic; they tend to accumulate quietly through repeated choices that alter the portfolio's intended shape, raise costs, or increase risk in ways that are easy to miss until performance disappoints. This is why the next discussion focuses on the practical mistakes investors make once they begin selecting and using ETFs in earnest.

Chasing performance and reacting to headlines

Chasing performance usually begins with a simple observation: a fund that has done well recently feels safer than one that has lagged. That feeling is powerful because recent returns are easy to see, easy to compare, and easy to mistake for evidence of future strength. In ETF investing, however, a short stretch of outperformance often tells you more about the market environment than about the fund itself. A sector ETF can surge because its industry is temporarily favored, a style ETF can lead because the economic cycle happens to reward its factor exposure, and a thematic ETF can rise because the story around it has captured investor attention. None of those outcomes guarantees that the same pattern will continue. Prices already reflect expectations, and markets have a way of reducing the advantage of what has become widely recognized.

This is where performance chasing becomes costly. Investors often buy after a strong run because the fund feels validated, then sell after a weak period because the same fund suddenly feels disappointing. The result is a habit of buying high and selling low, even when the investor believes the opposite is happening. Research on market efficiency helps explain why this pattern is so difficult to avoid: when information is widely known and quickly reflected in prices, yesterday's winners are not automatically tomorrow's bargains [128]. A fund's recent return may be real, but the reason for that return may already be embedded in the price of the underlying holdings. By the time a headline makes the strategy sound obvious, much of the opportunity may already have been absorbed by the market.

Headlines intensify the problem because they compress a complex market story into a single emotional cue. A dramatic article about inflation, artificial intelligence, bank stress, energy shortages, or geopolitical conflict can create the impression that a particular ETF is the "right" response. Sometimes the connection is valid, but the leap from a news event to a portfolio decision is often too fast. Markets do not move only because of the latest headline; they move because investors continuously revise expectations, and those revisions can happen before the public narrative catches up. The danger is not that news is irrelevant. The danger is that investors treat the news cycle as if it were a trading signal rather than one input among many.

ETF investors are especially vulnerable to this behavior because the product structure makes switching easy. A few clicks can move money from one fund to another, and that convenience can encourage the illusion that portfolio change is a low-friction way to respond to every new development. But an ETF is still a portfolio of underlying assets, and the decision to buy one should rest on the exposure it provides, the role it plays, and the risks it introduces. If a fund is purchased only because it is near the top of a recent performance table, the investor may be selecting the result rather than the process. That distinction matters because results are temporary, while the process determines whether the holding fits the rest of the portfolio.

One useful discipline is to ask what explains the performance before asking whether to buy it. If a broad market ETF has outperformed, the reason may be straightforward: the entire market has been strong. If a narrower ETF has outperformed, the reason may be much more specific: a single sector, region, or factor has had a favorable run. In that case, the fund may already be more expensive, more concentrated, or more crowded than it was when the opportunity first appeared. The investor should also consider whether the return came from a repeatable exposure or from a temporary market condition. A good ETF can have a bad year, and a poor ETF can have a great one. Recent returns alone do not tell you which is which.

Headline-driven buying also tends to ignore the difference between a short-term event and a long-term thesis. A news item may justify a tactical adjustment, but a tactical adjustment is not the same as a permanent portfolio change. If an investor wants to make a temporary shift, that decision should be tied to a clear time horizon and a defined reason for reversing course later. Otherwise, the portfolio can become a collection of reactions, each one made in response to the last market surprise. Over time, that pattern can create unnecessary turnover, higher trading costs, and a portfolio that no longer resembles the one originally designed. Even when the ETF itself is low cost, repeated trading can erode the benefit of that low cost.

There is also a behavioral trap in assuming that a widely discussed theme must be underowned or still early in its cycle. Popularity does not always mean excessive valuation, but it often means that expectations have already risen. In that setting, an investor may be buying a story that has become more fully priced than it appears from the outside. Some academic work on product design and indexing has also highlighted that what looks passive on the surface can still involve meaningful trading and timing effects at the margins [129]. That is another reason to avoid treating ETF ownership as a substitute for judgment. The wrapper may be efficient, but the investor still has to decide whether the exposure is worth owning now, at this price, for this purpose.

A more durable approach is to use performance and headlines as prompts for investigation, not as reasons for action by themselves. Strong recent returns can lead you to examine whether a fund's methodology, concentration, and risk profile still match your objectives. A major news event can lead you to test whether your current portfolio has a genuine vulnerability that needs attention. But the final decision should come from the portfolio plan, not from the emotional force of the latest market narrative. When investors slow down long enough to separate signal from excitement, they are less likely to mistake temporary leadership for lasting merit and less likely to turn every headline into a trade.

Overlapping holdings and false diversification

Overlapping holdings are one of the easiest ways for an ETF portfolio to look broader than it really is. This happens when several funds own many of the same underlying securities, so the investor believes they have diversified across multiple products while the portfolio is still carrying concentrated exposure to the same names, sectors, or factors. The issue is not limited to obvious duplicates. Two funds can have different labels, different indexes, and different expense ratios, yet still share a large core of holdings. That overlap matters because diversification is about the sources of return and risk in the portfolio, not the number of funds on the statement.

The problem often begins with well-intentioned fund selection. An investor may own a large-cap U.S. equity ETF, a growth ETF, a technology ETF, and a dividend ETF, expecting each to add a distinct layer of diversification. In practice, those funds may all hold the same dominant mega-cap stocks, only with slightly different weights. The portfolio then becomes more sensitive to the same market drivers than the investor realizes. A setback in a handful of large companies, or a rotation away from one style group, can affect several positions at once. The portfolio appears diversified because it contains multiple tickers, but the underlying economic exposure is still clustered.

This is why false diversification is such a persistent risk in ETF investing. The wrapper can create a sense of breadth that is not supported by the holdings. Investors often focus on the fund category rather than the overlap among the securities inside the funds. Broad market ETFs, sector ETFs, and style ETFs can all be useful on their own, but when combined without checking their holdings, they may produce redundant exposure. Academic work on index construction has shown that "index investing" is not a single uniform category and that benchmarks themselves can differ substantially in composition and design [10]. That heterogeneity means two funds that seem complementary on the surface may still be built around the same underlying engines of return.

False diversification is especially common when investors build portfolios by adding the "best" fund from each recent performance category. A strong-performing technology ETF, a momentum ETF, and a growth ETF may each seem like separate ideas, but they can all be heavily exposed to the same high-valuation stocks and the same market narrative. The portfolio then compounds the very risk the investor meant to avoid. Similar overlap can occur with bond ETFs as well. Several fixed-income funds may all hold the same broad duration profile or similar credit quality, giving the appearance of variety while leaving interest rate sensitivity largely unchanged.

The practical danger is that overlap can distort risk management. If an investor believes three or four funds represent separate sources of return, they may take on more total equity risk, more sector concentration, or more factor exposure than intended. Rebalancing becomes less effective when the holdings are not truly distinct, because trimming one fund may not reduce the underlying exposure as much as expected. Overlap also makes it harder to evaluate performance. When several funds own much of the same portfolio, it becomes difficult to tell whether a position is adding value or simply echoing the rest of the account.

Investors can reduce this problem by looking through the ticker to the actual holdings. The first question is whether the funds serve different portfolio roles. A broad U.S. market ETF and an international developed-market ETF may overlap very little and can work well together. A broad U.S. market ETF and a large-cap growth ETF may overlap heavily and may not justify separate positions unless the investor explicitly wants that tilt. The second question is whether the overlap is intentional. Some duplication is acceptable when it is part of a deliberate design, such as combining a core market fund with a smaller thematic or factor satellite. The problem is not overlap by itself; the problem is overlap that is not recognized, measured, or justified.

A useful discipline is to ask what new exposure each ETF actually brings to the portfolio. If the answer is mostly "more of what I already own," then the fund may not be adding diversification in any meaningful sense. This is where holdings analysis is more informative than fund labels. A portfolio built with awareness of overlap can be simpler, more coherent, and easier to manage than one that owns many funds but little additional breadth. In ETF investing, diversification is not achieved by multiplying products. It is achieved by combining exposures that behave differently when markets change.

Ignoring liquidity, structure, or index methodology

An ETF can still be a poor choice even when the headline cost is low and the fund appears easy to trade. The reason is that the wrapper does not determine the quality of the exposure by itself. What matters is the combination of the fund's liquidity profile, its structure, and the index or strategy it follows. Those elements shape how the ETF behaves in real use, especially when the market is stressed or when an investor needs to enter or exit a position quickly. A fund that looks efficient on a screen can become less attractive once those deeper features are examined.

Liquidity is often the first point of confusion. Investors may look at a fund's average daily volume and assume that number fully describes how easy it will be to trade. In reality, ETF liquidity is layered. The shares may trade actively on the exchange, but the underlying holdings may be far less liquid. In calm conditions, that distinction may not matter much. In volatile conditions, however, it can affect spreads, execution quality, and the size of the premium or discount at which shares trade. A large ETF holding highly liquid large-cap stocks is generally easier to transact in than a similar-sized ETF holding thinly traded bonds, small-cap securities, or niche exposures. The trading venue may be the same, but the market depth behind the fund is not.

Structure matters for the same reason. Some ETFs are built around straightforward, transparent, rules-based indexes. Others use sampling, derivatives, custom baskets, or active decision-making inside the fund. None of those structures is automatically wrong, but they are not interchangeable. A simple index fund generally makes it easier to understand what you own and how the portfolio is likely to behave. A more complex structure may introduce additional judgment, counterparty exposure, or operational moving parts that are less visible to the investor. Academic work has shown that "index" investing is not a single uniform category; the underlying indices themselves can differ substantially in design and behavior [10]. That means the label alone tells you less than many investors assume.

Index methodology is the blueprint that converts a market idea into a portfolio. Two funds can both claim to track the same asset class and still produce meaningfully different outcomes if one uses market-cap weighting, another applies screens, and a third rebalances on a different schedule. Methodology determines what enters the fund, what leaves it, how heavily each holding is weighted, and how concentrated the portfolio becomes over time. It also affects turnover and the degree to which the fund may be forced to buy high or sell low as constituents move in and out of eligibility. In benchmark-driven investing, the benchmark is not merely a label; it is a governing rule set, and that rule set has consequences for performance and risk [11].

This is why a fund's name should never be treated as a complete description of its behavior. A broad market ETF may appear to offer neutral exposure, yet the index behind it may have implicit tilts toward larger companies, certain sectors, or specific countries. A factor ETF may be marketed as a refined version of market exposure, but the factor definition itself can vary from sponsor to sponsor. Even funds that seem similar can differ in how often they rebalance, how they handle corporate actions, or how they respond when a security becomes hard to trade. Those differences can be subtle in a rising market and more visible when conditions tighten. Passive vehicles are increasingly important in capital markets, but their growing scale does not make them uniform or risk-free [2].

For investors, the practical issue is not whether liquidity, structure, or methodology are interesting in the abstract. It is whether they fit the role the ETF is meant to play. A core holding intended to sit in a portfolio for years can tolerate a different set of characteristics than a tactical position meant to be traded quickly. A broad equity ETF and a narrow commodity or sector ETF may both be exchange-traded, but one may be far more sensitive to trading frictions or benchmark design than the other. This matters because the cost of a poor fit is often invisible at the moment of purchase. It shows up later as slippage, tracking surprises, or a portfolio that behaves differently from what the investor expected.

There is also a broader market effect worth recognizing. As passive and index-linked assets have grown, they have become an important force in capital allocation and market structure [2]. That does not mean every ETF distorts prices or that index investing is inherently problematic. It does mean that the mechanics behind the fund deserve attention. In some markets, especially where liquidity is limited or the underlying assets are less standardized, index-linked products can interact with market conditions in ways that are not obvious from the ticker alone. For that reason, the investor's job is not simply to ask whether an ETF is cheap or popular. It is to ask what it owns, how it gets that exposure, and how reliably that exposure can be bought, held, and sold when needed.

Overtrading, poor rebalancing, and emotional decision-making

Overtrading usually begins with a portfolio that is already acceptable and then gets "improved" too often. An investor sees a market move, a news item, or a short-term performance gap and responds with a trade that changes the portfolio more than the underlying thesis has changed. With ETFs, this can happen easily because the instrument is simple to buy and sell, and the range of available funds makes it tempting to fine-tune every perceived problem. But each extra trade adds friction: spreads, commissions if applicable, possible tax consequences, and the risk of mistiming the market. Even when the explicit trading cost is small, repeated turnover can erode the disciplined structure that made the portfolio workable in the first place.

The danger is not limited to cost. Overtrading often turns a long-term allocation into a sequence of short-term opinions. An investor who began with a broad market core may start replacing one ETF after another based on recent headlines, temporary factor leadership, or the latest forecast about interest rates, inflation, or sector rotation. The result is often a portfolio that looks active but is actually reactive. Because ETFs make it easy to express a view in a single trade, they can encourage a false sense of control: the investor feels engaged, yet the portfolio may become less coherent and more dependent on timing skill that is rarely reliable over time. Passive investors in particular can fall into this trap when they confuse monitoring with constant intervention [2].

Poor rebalancing is a different mistake, but it can produce a similarly unstable portfolio. Rebalancing is meant to restore the intended relationship among asset classes, risk levels, and portfolio roles after markets have moved. When it is done poorly, either too often or too rarely, the portfolio drifts away from its design. Rebalancing too frequently can create unnecessary turnover and force the investor to sell recent winners and buy recent laggards before the portfolio has materially deviated from target. Rebalancing too infrequently can allow a portfolio to become more aggressive or more conservative than intended, depending on which assets have outperformed. The issue is not that rebalancing is optional; it is that it should be governed by a rule, not by mood.

There is also a more subtle problem: investors sometimes rebalance the wrong thing. They may focus on the number of funds rather than the exposures those funds represent. If several ETFs overlap heavily, a mechanical rebalance can preserve the appearance of balance while leaving the real risk profile unchanged. Likewise, if a portfolio includes a core index fund and a narrow satellite position, rebalancing should respect the different purposes of those holdings. The core may be allowed to remain the anchor, while the satellite may need tighter limits because it is meant to be smaller and more speculative. Rebalancing works best when the investor knows what each holding is supposed to do and measures drift against that purpose, not just against a table of percentages.

Emotional decision-making is the force that often connects overtrading and poor rebalancing. Fear tends to appear after declines, when investors want to reduce risk immediately, sell what has fallen, or abandon a strategy that no longer feels comfortable. Greed appears after gains, when recent winners seem more trustworthy than the plan that selected them in the first place. In ETF portfolios, both emotions are amplified by the visibility of intraday prices and by the ease of trading. A market screen can turn a temporary loss into a feeling of urgency, even when the portfolio's long-term structure has not changed. This is one reason disciplined implementation matters as much as fund selection: the best ETF choice can still be undermined by the investor's reaction to short-term noise.

Behavioral research in investing has repeatedly shown that decision quality falls when people rely too heavily on recent outcomes, vivid stories, or simplified narratives instead of a stable process. In practice, that means investors may sell a diversified ETF after a disappointing quarter, add to a thematic fund after a strong run, or move between styles based on whichever category has led most recently. The challenge is not merely emotional weakness; it is that markets reward patience unevenly, so a good process can feel wrong for long stretches. That is why rules matter. Rebalancing bands, calendar-based review dates, and pre-set position limits reduce the need to improvise under stress and help keep behavior aligned with the portfolio's original risk budget.

A useful discipline is to separate review from action. Reviewing a portfolio means checking whether the original assumptions still hold: time horizon, risk tolerance, cash needs, and the intended role of each ETF. Action should follow only when those assumptions have changed or when the portfolio has drifted far enough from target to justify a rebalance. This separation helps prevent the common habit of treating every market movement as a reason to trade. It also creates a better standard for evaluating thematic, factor, or sector ETFs, which are especially vulnerable to emotional buying and selling because their narratives are easy to understand and their price swings can be dramatic. Some of the most heavily marketed "ideas" in the ETF market are also the easiest to overtrade.

For many investors, the best safeguard is to make the portfolio harder to disrupt. That can mean using a written policy that defines target allocations, acceptable drift ranges, and the circumstances under which a trade is justified. It can also mean limiting portfolio checks to a regular schedule unless a real life event changes the plan. The goal is not to eliminate judgment, but to reserve it for decisions that genuinely matter. ETFs are efficient tools, but efficiency does not protect an investor from impatience. When trading becomes a substitute for discipline, the portfolio may still look diversified and modern on the surface while quietly losing the stability it was meant to provide.

Citations

The following sources were referenced in the preceding chapters. Each entry links back to the inline reference in the text. All sources were verified against the OpenAlex academic database at the time of generation.

OECD, OECD (2010). OECD Economics Department Working Papers . https://doi.org/10.1787/18151973 Jill E. Fisch, Asaf Hamdani, Steven Davidoff Solomon (2019). The New Titans of Wall Street: A Theoretical Framework for Passive Investors . https://openalex.org/W3217400049 Samuel A. Vigne, Brian M. Lucey, Fergal A. O'Connor et al. (2017). The financial economics of white precious metals — A survey . https://doi.org/10.1016/j.irfa.2017.04.006 Sebastian Steuer, Tobias Tröger (2022). The Role of Disclosure in Green Finance . https://doi.org/10.1093/jfr/fjac001 Wojtek Buczynski, Fabio Cuzzolin, Barbara J. Sahakian (2021). A review of machine learning experiments in equity investment decision-making: why most published research findings do not live up to their promise in real life . https://doi.org/10.1007/s41060-021-00245-5 Fernando García, Jairo González-Bueno, Francisco Guijarro et al. (2020). MULTIOBJECTIVE APPROACH TO PORTFOLIO OPTIMIZATION IN THE LIGHT OF THE CREDIBILITY THEORY . https://doi.org/10.3846/tede.2020.13189 Lin Lin (2022). Venture Capital in the Rise of Sustainable Investment . https://doi.org/10.1007/s40804-021-00238-8 Jun Gao, Niall O'Sullivan, Meadhbh Sherman (2021). Chinese securities investment funds: the role of luck in performance . https://doi.org/10.1108/raf-07-2020-0182 Charoula Daskalaki, George Skiadopoulos, Nikolas Topaloglou (2017). Diversification benefits of commodities: A stochastic dominance efficiency approach . https://doi.org/10.1016/j.jempfin.2017.07.004 Adriana Robertson (2019). Passive in Name Only: Delegated

Management and 'Index' Investing . https://openalex.org/W2902977516 Laurence B. Siegel, Barclay Douglas, Clifford Asness et al. (2003). Benchmarks and Investment Management . https://doi.org/10.2470/rf.v2003.n1.3922 Stephen Smith, David Hess, Cindy Maisannes et al. (2009). Investing Separately in Alpha and Beta . https://doi.org/10.2470/rf.v2009.n3 Bank for International Settlements (2006). Developing Corporate Bond Markets in Asia . https://doi.org/10.2139/ssrn.1188782 Melissa Vergara-Fernández, Conrad Heilmann, Marta Szymanowska (2023). Contextualist model evaluation: models in financial economics and index funds . https://doi.org/10.1007/s13194-022-00506-5 Ingo Walter, Robert D. Arnott, Theodore Aronson et al. (2015). The Industrial Organization of the Global Asset Management Business . https://doi.org/10.2470/rf.v2015.n5.1 Donald Chambers, Keith Black, Nelson Lacey et al. (2018). Alternative Investments: A Primer for Investment Professionals . https://doi.org/10.2470/rf.v2018.n1.1 Faleh M. F. E. Alrashidi (2013). COMPARISON OF THE PERFORMANCE OF ISLAMIC MUTUAL FUNDS vs. ETHICAL AND CONVENTIONAL MUTUAL FUNDS . https://openalex.org/W28375514 M. Klimova (2022). Potential Effects of ESG (Environmental, Social, and Governance) Policies on the Returns of an Investment Portfolio . https://doi.org/10.26794/2308-944x-2022-10-2-21-55 Anni Salo (2017). Robo advisor, your reliable partner? Building a trustworthy digital investment management service . https://openalex.org/W2765955082 Syed Kumail Abbas Rizvi, Bushra Naqvi, Nawazish Mirza (2021). Is green investment different from grey? Return and volatility spillovers between green and grey energy ETFs . https://doi.org/10.1007/s10479-021-04367-8 Jan Fichtner, Robin Jaspert, Johannes Petry (2023). Mind the ESG capital allocation gap: The role of index providers, standard-setting, and “green” indices for the creation of sustainability impact . https://doi.org/10.1111/rego.12530 Bilal Hassan Ahmed Khattak, Imran Shafi, Abdul Saboor

Khan et al. (2023). A Systematic Survey of AI Models in Financial Market Forecasting for Profitability Analysis . https://doi.org/10.1109/access.2023.3330156 Georg Inderst, Christopher Kaminker, Fiona Stewart (2012). Defining and Measuring Green Investments . https://doi.org/10.1787/5k9312twnn44-en Aneesh Raghunandan, Shiva Rajgopal (2022). Do ESG funds make stakeholder-friendly investments? . https://doi.org/10.1007/s11142-022-09693-1 Claudio Raddatz, Sergio L. Schmukler, Tomás Williams (2017). International asset allocations and capital flows: The benchmark effect . https://doi.org/10.1016/j.jinteco.2017.06.007 Helena Naffa, Máté Fain (2020). Performance measurement of ESG-themed megatrend investments in global equity markets using pure factor portfolios methodology . https://doi.org/10.1371/journal.pone.0244225 Xing Chen, Bert Scholtens (2018). The urge to act: A comparison of active and passive socially responsible investment funds in the United States . https://doi.org/10.1002/csr.1529 Carla Henriques, Maria Elisabete Neves, Licínio Castelão et al. (2022). Assessing the performance of exchange traded funds in the energy sector: a hybrid DEA multiobjective linear programming approach . https://doi.org/10.1007/s10479-021-04323-6 Andrew deWaard (2024). Derivative Media: How Wall Street Devours Culture . https://doi.org/10.1525/luminos.197 Alain Wouassom (2017). Momentum and Contrarian Trading Strategies: Implication for Risk-sharing and Informational Efficiency of Security Markets . https://openalex.org/W2743031960 Twum-Darko, Michael, Matsoso, Mamorena (2015). Proceedings of the 7th International Conference on Business and Finance . https://doi.org/10.4102/aosis.7icbf.2015.02 Keith MacMaster (2018). Responsible Investing: Access Denied . https://openalex.org/W2889277425 Paul Tucker, Michael Haliassos, Theodor Kockelkoren et al. (2015). Challenges in Securities Markets Regulation: Investor Protection and Corporate Governance . https://openalex.org/

W2251402821 Victor R. Baker (2021). Employment Discrimination: An Efficacy Study of African American Inequities in the California Utility Sector . https://openalex.org/W3206806052 Joel Krupa (2019). The Intersection of Renewable Energy Finance and Governance: Solutions to the Multi-trillion Dollar Challenges . https://openalex.org/W3154770532 Oluwole Solanke (2014). Organizational effectiveness in higher education: a case study of selected polytechnics in Nigeria . https://openalex.org/W1493367538 OECD (2017). Common Ownership by Institutional Investors and its Impact on Competition . https://doi.org/10.1787/40c7872a-en Vaibhav Chaturvedi, Arunabha Ghosh, Amit Garg et al. (2024). India's pathway to net zero by 2070: status, challenges, and way forward . https://doi.org/10.1088/1748-9326/ad7749 Athanasios G. Panagopoulos, Ioannis Tzionas (2023). The Use of Sustainable Financial Instruments in Relation to the Social Impact Investment: ESG Policies, Capital Markets' Approach and Investors' Protection: An Innovative Perspective for a Global Surveillance Authority . https://doi.org/10.5430/ijba.v14n1p87 Nini Johana Marín-Rodríguez, Juan David González-Ruíz, Sergio Botero-Botero (2025). Towards New Strategies for Investing: Insights on Sustainable Exchange-Traded Funds (ETFs) . https://doi.org/10.3390/world6010008 OECD (2023). Towards Orderly Green Transntion . https://doi.org/10.1787/24520e7e-en Andres Vinelli, N Amenc, G Bruno et al. (2024). Smart Beta, Direct Indexing, and Index-Based Investment Strategies: A Framework . https://doi.org/10.56227/24.1.16 Asian Development Bank (2017). Catalyzing Green Finance: . https://doi.org/10.22617/tcs178941 Rinay Bhownath (2017). Headline differences between sector valuations on the Johannesburg Stock Exchange : market timing opportunities . https://openalex.org/W2916547597 Jaakko Aspara, Risto Rajala, Virpi Kristiina Tuunainen (2012). The future of banking services . https://openalex.org/W2603491024 Mona A. ElBannan (2023). Returns behavior of ESG

ETFs in the COVID-19 market crash: Are green funds more resilient? . https://doi.org/10.1002/jcaf.22680 Franklin Allen, Xian Gu, Julapa Jagtiani (2020). A Survey of Fintech Research and Policy Discussion . https://doi.org/10.21799/frbp.wp.2020.21 John Coates (2009). Reforming the Taxation and Regulation of Mutual Funds: A Comparative Legal and Economic Analysis . https://doi.org/10.1093/jla/1.2.591 Gerald R. Jensen, Jeffrey M. Mercer, I Wylie et al. (2011). Commodities as an Investment . https://doi.org/10.2470/rflr.v6.n2.1 Ya Dai, Liang Guo, Steve Liu et al. (2022). Are socially responsible exchange-traded funds paying off in performance? . https://doi.org/10.1111/irfi.12389 Olga Balakina, Claes Bäckman, Andreas Hackethal et al. (2022). Good Peers, Good Apples? Peer Effects in Portfolio Quality . https://doi.org/10.2139/ssrn.4150243 Patrick Velte (2021). Meta-analyses on Corporate Social Responsibility (CSR): a literature review . https://doi.org/10.1007/s11301-021-00211-2 Priya Malhotra (2024). The rise of passive investing: a systematic literature review applying PRISMA framework . https://doi.org/10.1108/jcms-12-2023-0046 OECD (2020). ESG Investing . https://doi.org/10.1787/5504598c-en Byungguk Ko, Kyu-Hwan Lee, Yong-Beum Yoon et al. (2022). Impact of ESG (Environmental, Social, Governance) on the Performance of Electric Utilities . https://doi.org/10.7849/ksnre.2022.0010 Balázs Stempler (2021). ESG Investing: The Use of ESG Ratings in a Smart Beta Strategy . https://doi.org/10.33893/fer.20.2.91116 Andreas G. F. Hoepner, Paolo Masoni, Brenda Kramer (2018). TEG Final Report on Climate Benchmarks and Benchmarks' ESG Disclosure . https://openalex.org/W3102910239 Williams Chibueze Munonye, Daniella Ifunanya Munonye (2026). Beyond greenwashing: how circular economy metrics could revolutionize ESG investing . https://doi.org/10.3389/frsus.2025.1588374 Salvatore Carta, Sergio Consoli, Alessandro Sebastian Podda et al. (2021). Ensembling and Dynamic Asset Selection for Risk-

Controlled Statistical Arbitrage . https://doi.org/10.1109/access.2021.3059187 Yu Wang (2011). Information Content of Mutual Fund Portfolio Disclosure . https://openalex.org/W1576720825 Frantz Maurer, S. Owen Williams (2014). Physically Versus Synthetically Replicated Trackers: Is There A Difference In Terms Of Risk? . https://doi.org/10.19030/jabr.v31i1.8996 Ian Ayres, Quinn Curtis (2014). Beyond Diversification: The Pervasive Problem of Excessive Fees and 'Dominated Funds' in 401(k) Plans . https://doi.org/10.2139/ssrn.2399531 Christian A.M. Wilson, Ben Caldecott (2021). Breaking the Bond: Primary Markets and Carbon-Intensive Financing . https://doi.org/10.2139/ssrn.3883377 Mila Getmansky, Peter Lee, Andrew W. Lo (2015). Hedge Funds: A Dynamic Industry In Transition . https://doi.org/10.3386/w21449 José Manuel Santos Jaén, Gema Martín de Almagro-Vázquez, María del Carmen Valls Martínez (2023). Is earnings management impacted by audit fees and auditor tenure? An analysis of the Big Four audit firms in the US market . https://doi.org/10.24136/oc.2023.027 Söhnke M. Bartram, Harald Lohre, Peter F. Pope et al. (2021). Navigating the factor zoo around the world: an institutional investor perspective . https://doi.org/10.1007/s11573-021-01035-y World Bank (2020). Climate Change in APEC: Assessing Risks, Preparing Financial Markets, and Mobilizing Institutional Investors . https://doi.org/10.1596/33423 Subhash D. Pawar, . . (2024). Fintech Innovation as a Catalyst for India's Financial Services Transformation (From 2016 to 2023) . https://doi.org/10.17010/ijrcm/2024/v11i4/174725 Vidhan K. Goyal, Daniel Urban, Wenting Zhao (2025). Index Creation, Information Changes, and Financing* . https://doi.org/10.1111/1475-679x.12626 Alan Fernandez, Remy Kaldawy, Zoraver Kang et al. (2019). AI Driven System of Trading Systems . https://openalex.org/W2970448025 Igor Pouchkarev (2005). Performance Evaluation of Constrained Portfolios . https://openalex.org/W2165669276 David Puelz (2018). Regularization in econometrics and finance . https://doi.org/10.15781/t2r20sd9t Cornelius Francois Lombard (2015). Decision-making under uncertainty : Markowitz optimisation as a passive strategy on the JSE . https://openalex.org/W2593174285 Tobias H. Troeger, Sebastian Steuer (2021). The Role of Disclosure in Green Finance . https://doi.org/10.2139/ssrn.3908617 Ragnar Gudmundarson, Gareth W. Peters (2024). Assessing portfolio diversification via two-sample graph kernel inference. A case study on the influence of ESG screening . https://doi.org/10.1371/journal.pone.0301804 Unknown author (2022). Global ESG Disclosure Standards for Investment Products . https://doi.org/10.56227/24.3.1 Antonio J. Hidalgo-Marín, Antonio J. Nebro, José García-Nieto (2025). Efficient Selection of Investment Portfolios in Real-World Markets: A Multi-Objective Optimization Approach . https://doi.org/10.3390/a19010020 OECD (2022). Supporting women's empowerment through green policies and finance . https://doi.org/10.1787/16771957-en Sait Abdulah, Muhamad Syauqillah, Jerry Marcellinus et al. (2020). – The Asian Conference on the Social Sciences 2020: Official Conference Proceedings . https://doi.org/10.22492/issn.2186-2303.2020 Gabriela Prelipcean, Mircea Boşcoianu (2020). Risk Analysis of a Hedge Fund Oriented on Sustainable and Responsible Investments for Emerging Markets . https://doi.org/10.24818/ea/2020/55/653 Tewogbade Lateefat, Folake Ajoke Bankole (2021). Capital Allocation Strategies in Asset Management Firms to Maximize Efficiency and Support Growth Objectives . https://doi.org/10.54660/.ijmrge.2021.2.2.478-495 Vsevolod Isakov (2019). Performance appraisal of exchange-traded funds using clustering and data envelopment analysis (XETRA, Germany) . https://openalex.org/W2951159573 Medhanie Mekonnen (2017). Relationship between Mutual Fund Type, Portfolio Turnover, Longevity, Management Turnover, and Performance . https://openalex.org/W2765635355 Anne

Merrild Hansen, Pelle Tejsner, Parnuna Petrina Egede (2016). Traditional Knowledge and Industrial Development: On the potential use of indigenous and local knowledge as a resource to assess competencies in Greenland . https://openalex.org/W2598784042 Henning Salling Olesen (2017). The Concept of Competence and the Challenge of Competence Assessment . https://openalex.org/W2808433508 Justus Inhoffen (2025). Essays on Interconnected Markets . https://doi.org/10.5463/thesis.1011 Ronald G. Sultana, Anna Spiteri, David Ashton et al. (2002). Vocational education and training and employment services in Malta . https://openalex.org/W3033639032 Helen Ding, Courtney Nina McLaren (2025). Financial Sector Guidebook on Nature-Based Solutions Investment: Aligning Investment With Impacts and Showcasing Examples . https://doi.org/10.46830/wrigb.24.00043 Gerald Lee House (2020). Financial Advisory Firms' Strategies for Diversifying and Growing Clients' Portfolio . https://openalex.org/W3044645413 Unknown author (2013). Manager Selection . https://doi.org/10.2470/rf.v2013.n4.1 Michael Toulch (2018). Ecolabels: On the Money? A Policy Evaluation of Eco-labels for Retail Investment Products in the EU . https://openalex.org/W2932848233 Blitz, D.C. (David) (2001). Benchmarking the Benchmarks . https://doi.org/10.1300/j162v02n03_01 Bárbara Weber, Mirjam Staub-Bisang, Hans Wilhelm Alfen et al. (2016). Infrastructure Investments . https://doi.org/10.1002/9781119226574.ch2 Josh Lerner, James Tighe, Steve Dew et al. (2016). Impact of Early Stage Equity Funds in Latin America . https://doi.org/10.18235/0006474 Cristiana Tudor, Alexandra Horobeţ, Zeno Dinca et al. (2026). Investment implications of Industry 4.0: evidence from smart manufacturing ETFs . https://doi.org/10.3846/jbem.2026.25512 Mahan Tahvildari (2026). An Analysis and Improvement of Robo-Advisory . https://openalex.org/W7134867016 Michaela Dorocáková (2017). Comparison of ETF´s performance related to the tracking error . https://

doi.org/10.14254/2071-8330.2017/10-4/12 Nicole Maria Namyslo, Dominik Jung, Timo Sturm (2025). The state of robo-advisory design: A systematic consolidation of design requirements and recommendations . https://doi.org/10.1007/s12525-025-00762-2 Beerbaum, Dirk, Julia M. Puaschunder (2019). A Behavioral Approach to Irrational Exuberances – An Artificial Intelligence Roboethics Taxonomy . https://doi.org/10.5281/zenodo.3355683 Mehmet Gülşen, Burak Yıldız (2024). An algorithmic approach to portfolio construction: A Turkish stock market case . https://doi.org/10.1016/j.bir.2024.10.002 Michael Heinrich Baumann, Michaela Baumann, Bernhard Herz (2020). Are ETFs Bad for Financial Health . https://openalex.org/W3096892092 Manoel Fernando Alonso Gadi, Maximilian Schmidt, Noah Ruemmele et al. (2024). An empirical approach and practical framework for a decentralized Ethereum Ecosystem Index (EEI) . https://doi.org/10.7717/peerj-cs.1766 David Hendel (2025). Systemic Forces in Software: Macroeconomic Sensitivity, Risk Concentration, and Portfolio Construction in the Global Software Equity Market . https://doi.org/10.58445/rars.3056 Muhammad Abubakr Naeem, Sitara Karim, Larisa Yarovaya et al. (2023). COVID-induced sentiment and the intraday volatility spillovers between energy and other ETFs . https://doi.org/10.1016/j.eneco.2023.106677 María del Rosario Venegas, Jorge Feregrino Feregrino, Nelson David Lay Raby et al. (2024). Food Financialization: Impact of Derivatives and Index Funds on Agri-Food Market Volatility . https://doi.org/10.3390/ijfs12040121 Xiao-Yang Liu, Ziyi Xia, Hongyang Yang et al. (2024). Dynamic datasets and market environments for financial reinforcement learning . https://doi.org/10.1007/s10994-023-06511-w Nikoletta Poutachidou, Alexandros Koulis (2025). The Investment Styles and Performance of AI-Related ETFs: Analyzing the Impact of Active Management . https://doi.org/10.3390/fintech4020020 Richard Harris, Murat Mazibaş, Dooruj Rambaccussing (2024). Bitcoin replication using machine learning .

https://doi.org/10.1016/j.irfa.2024.103207 Ian Ayres, Quinn Curtis (2015). PROTECTING CONSUMER INVESTORS BY FACILITATING "IMPROVED PERFORMANCE" COMPETITION . https://openalex.org/W2215066497 Vidar Kogstad Nygaard (2016). Time-series and cross-sectional price momentum : an empirical study at the Oslo stock exchange . https://openalex.org/W2593050226 Ramezanifar (2018). Investment is style and strategy . https://doi.org/10.26481/dis.20180228er Andrew N. Smith (2014). Sensegiving Word-of-Mouth and Collective Sensemaking About Epistemic Objects . https://openalex.org/W2276813308 Marisa Alexandra Abreu Gonçalves (2016). Understanding the Trends of European Startup Ecosystems . https://openalex.org/W2616553562 Tom Gosling (2024). Universal Owners and Climate Change . https://doi.org/10.1093/jfr/fjae010 Tom Gosling (2024). Universal Owners and Climate Change . https://doi.org/10.2139/ssrn.4713536 Boris Fays, Marie Lambert, Nicolas Papageorgiou (2018). Smart Equity Investing: Implementing Risk Optimization Techniques on Strategic Beta Portfolios . https://openalex.org/W3096806952 Paul Rose (2013). Sovereign Investing and Corporate Governance: Evidence and Policy . https://openalex.org/W3123095550 A. Майти (2025). Эмпирический анализ паевых инвестиционных фондов на индийских финансовых рынках . https://openalex.org/W7140062624 Finn Christian Simonn (2025). Past, Present, and Future Research Trajectories on Retail Investor Behaviour: A Composite Bibliometric Analysis and Literature Review . https://doi.org/10.3390/ijfs13020105 Iqbal Owadally, Jean-René Mwizere, Neema Kalidas et al. (2021). Long-Term Sustainable Investment for Retirement . https://doi.org/10.3390/su13095000 Xavier Gabaix, Ralph S. J. Koijen, Federico Mainardi et al. (2023). Asset Demand of U.S. Households . https://doi.org/10.3386/w32001 Dewald Kellerman (2018). Analysing the investor life cycle in a South African universal bank . https://openalex.org/W2929820415

Joonas Haakana (2014). Smart Beta ETFs: Adding Value for the ETF Investors? . https://openalex.org/W108843276 Swastika Rajhununan (2024). The effect of economic uncertainty on exchange traded fund performance and volatility in South Africa. . https://openalex.org/W7135350545 Quynh Chi Tran (2019). Applying artificial intelligence in index tracking : case of the FTSE 100 index . https://openalex.org/W2993465644 Paul Smith, Robert C. Pozen, Suresh Nallareddy et al. (2018). Research Foundation Review 2017 . https://doi.org/10.2470/rf.v2018.n2.1 Ryan Clements (2020). Post-Crisis Financialization Through Product Innovation: Assessing Complexity, Growth & Design In Exchange Traded Funds . https://openalex.org/W3112595429 Bernd Schlusche (2010). Essays on the Efficiency of Financial Markets . https://openalex.org/W3214663169 Rob Arnott, Lillian Wu (2026). The Active Side of Indexing . https://doi.org/10.56227/26.1.9 Office of the Deputy Technical Governor, Office for Monetary Operations and International Investments, Sub-Directorate for Portfolio Management et al. (2026). Foreign Reserves Management 2025 . https://doi.org/10.32468/inf-adm-res-int.eng.2025 Fan Yang, Tomáš Havránek, Zuzana Iršová et al. (2023). Is research on hedge fund performance published selectively? A quantitative survey . https://doi.org/10.1111/joes.12574 Gerasimos G. Rompotis (2026). A Study on the Performance of Actively and Passively Managed Artificial Intelligence Exchange Traded Funds . https://doi.org/10.3390/jrfm19040267 Markus Hjulgren (2018). Factor Investing in Practice: Performance and Risk Exposure of U.S. Factor ETFs . https://openalex.org/W2945773468 Yaodong Zhang (2025). Three Papers on Heterogeneous Investors and Their Financial Market Implications . https://doi.org/10.25911/yky2-6171 Jean-Paul van Brakel (2026). Mutual fund behavior under the microscope . https://openalex.org/W7126761270 Evgeni Tarassov (2016). Exchange Traded Funds (ETF): history, mechanism, academic literature review and research perspectives .

https://doi.org/10.17323/j.jcfr.2073-0438.10.2.2016.89-108 Malayendu Saha, Anirban Hazra (2026). AI in the Emerging Economy Integrating Data, Decision, and Development . https://doi.org/10.65525/svup.9788199651586.2026.1-158 Nicolas Meng (2013). Optimal Portfolios: The Benefts of Advanced Techniques in Risk Management and Portfolio Optimization . https://doi.org/10.3929/ethz-a-009900690 Garofalo, Davide (2025). Strategic decision framework for tokenized funds in commercial banking : a business, technology, and risk perspective . https://openalex.org/W7112529576 Unknown author (2025). Proceedings of the International scientific conference "Modern Trends in the Development of Science and Society" . https://doi.org/10.64076/iedc251023

Conclusion

At some point, the investor's task stops being about comparing funds and becomes about maintaining a system. The system does not need to be elaborate, but it does need to be coherent enough that each ETF has a defined role, each role supports a broader objective, and each adjustment can be judged against a preexisting standard rather than a passing mood. That is where the discipline of ETF investing becomes most visible: not in the purchase itself, but in the habits that govern what happens afterward.

A durable ETF portfolio is usually built around a small number of recurring questions. Does this holding still serve the purpose for which it was selected? Has the portfolio drifted far enough from its intended structure that the balance of risk has changed? Are new contributions being directed in a way that reinforces the plan, or are they being used to chase whatever has recently performed best? These questions matter because ETFs make it easy to act quickly, and that convenience can be helpful only when it is matched by a clear decision framework.

One of the most useful habits is to separate the portfolio's design from its implementation. The design is the long-term allocation and the set of exposures the investor wants to own through different market environments. The implementation is the practical process of using ETFs to express that design. A sound design can still be undermined by poor implementation if the investor trades too often, ignores cost at the point of execution, or lets a satellite position grow into something larger than intended. Likewise, a modest design can be improved by careful implementation that keeps costs low, taxes manageable, and turnover restrained.

That distinction becomes especially important when markets are noisy. ETFs are often marketed as simple instruments, and in a narrow sense they are: they can be bought, sold, and held with little operational complexity. But simplicity at the transaction level should not be confused with simplicity at the portfolio level. A fund can be easy to trade and still create complexity if it overlaps with existing holdings, concentrates risk in a familiar-looking theme, or behaves differently from what the investor assumed. The better approach is to treat each ETF as one component in a larger structure whose purpose must be defended over time.

For many investors, the most effective portfolio maintenance is unglamorous. It involves periodic review rather than constant revision. It involves deciding in advance how often the portfolio will be checked, what deviations will trigger action, and which changes are worth making only when the underlying investment case has genuinely changed. This kind of structure reduces the temptation to react to every market move. It also helps prevent a common form of drift in which a portfolio slowly becomes more aggressive, more concentrated, or more expensive without the investor ever consciously choosing that outcome.

Rebalancing fits into that discipline, but it should not be mistaken for a mechanical ritual detached from purpose. A portfolio is rebalanced because the original mix of assets no longer reflects the intended balance of risk and return. That may happen after a strong rally in equities, a sharp rise in rates, or a prolonged period in which one segment of the market outpaces the rest. Rebalancing restores proportionality, but it can also be used as a way to make the portfolio behave more like the plan and less like recent history.

There is also a behavioral dimension to maintenance that deserves as much attention as the fund selection itself. Investors often think of risk in terms of what the market might do, but a great deal of portfolio damage comes from what the investor does in response. Selling after a decline, adding aggressively after a surge, or abandoning a disciplined allocation because a different strategy looks more exciting can all have lasting effects. Passive investment vehicles play a major role in capital markets, and their influence depends in part on whether investors use them as intended or treat them as temporary vehicles for emotion-driven decisions [2].

The same caution applies to specialized ETFs that promise a particular theme, factor, or objective. These funds can be useful when they are placed deliberately within a broader portfolio, but they should be monitored for concentration, style drift, and changing assumptions about the underlying thesis. A theme that seemed compelling when enthusiasm was high may turn out to be more cyclical, more crowded, or more narrowly dependent on a few companies than originally expected. In those cases, the question is not whether the fund is still fashionable, but whether it still earns its place in the portfolio.

Investors who use ETFs for values-based or sustainability-oriented exposure face an additional layer of scrutiny. The label alone does not guarantee that the holdings or voting behavior will align cleanly with the stated objective. Research on self-labelled ESG funds has found that stated intent and actual portfolio composition can diverge in meaningful ways [24]. Other work on disclosure and green finance underscores how important transparency is if market discipline is expected to do the work of sorting stronger claims from weaker ones [4]. For the investor, that means the review process should focus on holdings, methodology, and disclosure quality rather than on the fund's marketing language.

That same principle extends beyond ESG. Whether the ETF is broad-based, sector-specific, or built around a particular factor, the label should be treated as a starting point, not a conclusion. The real question is always what the fund owns, how it behaves, and what kind of portfolio role it can credibly fill. A portfolio built on that standard is less likely to be disrupted by product hype, short-term performance swings, or the appearance of a new fund that seems to offer the same exposure with a more appealing story.

In practice, the long-term value of ETF investing comes from consistency. Consistency does not mean rigidity; portfolios should adapt when goals change, time horizons shorten, or risk tolerance evolves. But consistency does mean that changes should be made for reasons the investor can explain clearly and would still defend after the market has moved again. That is the standard that turns ETFs from a convenient product category into a durable investment framework.

Appendix: ETF Research Checklist and Glossary

The material that follows is meant to serve as a working reference, not a substitute for judgment. By this point, the main questions are no longer abstract: the investor has enough context to compare funds, but still needs a disciplined way to organize the final review and a common vocabulary for what the review is actually measuring. That is the purpose of this appendix. It gathers the core items that should be checked before capital is committed, then defines the terms that tend to appear repeatedly in fund documents, fact sheets, and portfolio discussions. It also closes with a short set of questions that help turn a product screen into an informed decision. Used together, these tools make it easier to evaluate an ETF on its own terms rather than relying on a name, a theme, or a recent performance chart.

ETF evaluation checklist

A useful ETF review begins by asking whether the fund does what it says it does, at a cost and in a structure that fit the investor's purpose. The first check is the objective itself. The name of the fund should not be treated as a sufficient description of its behavior. A broad-market equity ETF, a dividend-focused ETF, and a low-volatility ETF may all appear to offer stock exposure, but each is built to solve a different problem. The investor should be able to state the fund's role in plain language: core equity exposure, bond ballast, sector tilt, income generation, inflation sensitivity, or a temporary implementation tool. If that role cannot be identified clearly, the fund is already difficult to evaluate.

After the objective comes the benchmark and the method used to follow it. The index or strategy is the blueprint, and the blueprint deserves close reading. An investor should know what securities are eligible, how they are weighted, how often the portfolio is reconstituted, and whether the fund uses screens based on value, quality, momentum, volatility, dividends, or other factors. Two ETFs can claim similar exposure while behaving differently because their underlying rules differ. That is especially important for specialized or thematic funds, where the label may be broader than the actual holdings. A disciplined review asks whether the methodology is transparent enough to understand and stable enough to trust.

Cost deserves more than a glance at the expense ratio. The published fee is important, but it is only one element of total ownership cost. Investors should also consider the bid-ask spread, likely trading frequency, and the possibility that a low-fee fund still becomes expensive if it is difficult to trade efficiently. In addition, the tax profile matters in taxable accounts. A fund that looks cheap on paper may be less attractive if it generates distributions that create unwanted tax consequences. A practical checklist therefore compares the stated fee with the full economic burden of owning the ETF, not simply the annual charge shown in the prospectus.

Liquidity and size should be evaluated carefully, but not mechanically. Assets under management can be a useful sign of market acceptance, yet it does not by itself guarantee efficient trading. Average trading volume matters, but it should be read alongside the liquidity of the underlying securities. A fund holding highly liquid large-cap stocks may trade efficiently even if its own volume is modest, while a fund built around thinly traded bonds or niche securities may be more sensitive to market stress. The question is not just whether the ETF trades, but how it is likely to behave when an investor needs to buy or sell in size. Recent portfolio research in risk management emphasizes that implementation details can materially affect realized outcomes, even when the strategic idea is sound [138].

Holdings deserve direct inspection. A fund should not be judged only by category label or marketing language; the actual portfolio tells the real story. Investors should look for concentration in a few names, sectors, or issuers, and they should ask whether that concentration is intentional or accidental. A portfolio that seems diversified at the ticker level can still be narrow in substance if it owns the same mega-cap stocks as several other funds already in the account. Overlap is especially important when combining multiple ETFs, because false diversification can leave the portfolio more exposed than expected. The holdings list also reveals whether the fund uses derivatives, cash substitutions, sampling, or full replication, each of which can affect tracking and risk.

Transparency and sponsor quality are the final structural checks. An ETF should disclose its holdings and methodology in a way that allows the investor to understand what is owned and how often it changes. That does not mean every fund must reveal every detail instantly, but it does mean the investor should not be forced to guess how the product works. The provider's reputation matters as well, particularly for operational reliability, index governance, trading support, and product stewardship. A fund from a well-run sponsor is not automatically superior, but a sponsor with weak disclosure, inconsistent communication, or a history of product confusion should raise caution. In practice, the checklist is less about finding a perfect ETF than about eliminating avoidable uncertainty before capital is committed.

One simple way to use the checklist is to ask whether each answer points in the same direction. If the objective is clear, the methodology is transparent, the cost is reasonable, the holdings are appropriate, and the liquidity profile matches the intended use, the fund is probably worth deeper consideration. If several answers conflict, the ETF may still be usable, but only if the investor understands the tradeoff being accepted. That discipline is what separates a fund that merely looks attractive from one that can be held with confidence through ordinary market noise and the more difficult periods when precision matters most.

Key terms and definitions

Some terms in ETF investing are used so often that they can seem interchangeable, but they are not. Precision matters because many of the judgments an investor makes depend on whether a term describes the fund's structure, its trading behavior, its portfolio contents, or its role in the market. A fund can be highly liquid without being low cost. It can be index-based without being passive in the ordinary sense of the word. It can be transparent in its holdings while still being difficult to understand in practice. Using the vocabulary carefully helps prevent one of the most common errors in fund analysis: assuming that a familiar label tells the whole story. That is especially important in a market where passive vehicles now direct enormous capital flows and have a growing influence on corporate ownership and governance [2].

Asset under management (AUM) is the total market value of the assets held by a fund. In ETF analysis, AUM is often used as a rough indicator of scale, but it should not be treated as a direct measure of quality. A large ETF may benefit from stronger trading activity, wider institutional use, and more stable operations, yet a smaller ETF can still be well designed and effective for a specific purpose. Average trading volume is different: it refers to how many shares change hands on the exchange over a given period, usually a day. Volume helps describe how active the secondary market is, but it does not fully capture the ease of trading the underlying securities. Liquidity is the broader concept. It refers to how easily a position can be bought or sold without causing a large price impact. In ETFs, liquidity exists at more than one level: the shares themselves, the securities inside the fund, and the market conditions that connect the two.

Bid-ask spread is the difference between the highest price a buyer is willing to pay and the lowest price a seller is willing to accept. It is one of the main trading frictions in ETF investing. A narrow spread usually signals efficient trading conditions, while a wide spread can make even a low-expense fund more costly to use. Premium and discount describe the relationship between an ETF's market price and its net asset value. If shares trade above net asset value, the ETF is at a premium; if they trade below it, the ETF is at a discount. These differences are often small in well-functioning markets, but they matter because they show that the share price is determined by supply and demand on the exchange, not by the fund's holdings alone.

Net asset value (NAV) is the per-share value of the ETF's underlying portfolio after liabilities are subtracted from assets. NAV is usually calculated once at the end of the trading day, and it serves as the accounting reference point for the fund. The market price of the ETF may move away from NAV during the day, which is why investors should not assume that the quoted share price is identical to the value of the underlying securities. Creation unit refers to the large block of ETF shares that authorized participants can create or redeem in the primary market. This mechanism helps keep market price and NAV close over time. Authorized participant means the institution that has the ability to exchange the underlying basket of assets, or a cash equivalent, for ETF shares directly with the fund sponsor. Most individual investors never interact with this process directly, but it is central to how ETFs function [10].

Index methodology is the rulebook that determines what belongs in the fund, how holdings are weighted, when the portfolio is rebalanced, and what screens or constraints apply. Two ETFs can both say they track the same market and still behave differently because their methodologies are not identical. Related terms such as cap-weighted, equal-weighted, factor-based, and screened describe the logic used to select and weight holdings. A cap-weighted index gives larger companies more influence. An equal-weighted index gives each holding the same starting weight. A factor-based ETF emphasizes characteristics such as value, momentum, quality, or low volatility. A screened ETF excludes or includes securities according to rules tied to sector, industry, sustainability, or other criteria. The growing use of ESG and green labels has made this distinction especially important, because disclosure and labeling do not always guarantee that the portfolio will produce the intended real-world effect [4][21][23].

Tracking difference is the gap between the ETF's return and the return of its benchmark over a stated period. Tracking error is the degree to which that gap varies over time. These terms are often confused, but they answer different questions. Tracking difference tells you whether the fund has generally lagged or outperformed the benchmark. Tracking error tells you how consistently it has done so. Expense ratio is the annual fee charged by the fund, expressed as a percentage of assets. It is deducted inside the fund and reduces return automatically. Total return includes price change plus distributions, while distribution refers to cash paid out by the fund, such as dividends, interest, or realized capital gains. Turnover measures how frequently the portfolio changes. Higher turnover can raise trading costs and, in taxable accounts, may increase the chance of taxable distributions.

Primary market and secondary market describe two different trading arenas. The primary market is where ETF shares are created or redeemed in large blocks. The secondary market is where ordinary investors buy and sell shares on the exchange. Underlying holdings are the securities the ETF actually owns, while exposure is the economic result those holdings are intended to deliver. That distinction matters because a fund's exposure can differ from the simple list of securities if derivatives, sampling methods, or other portfolio techniques are used. In the same way, replication means the method used to match the benchmark, whether by holding every security in the index or by using a representative sample. Finally, tax efficiency refers to the extent to which the fund minimizes taxable distributions and other tax costs for shareholders. In practice, these terms are not just definitions to memorize; they are the vocabulary used to compare whether one ETF is merely familiar, or actually suitable for the role it is meant to play.

Questions to ask before buying an ETF

Before buying an ETF, it helps to turn the decision into a sequence of plain questions rather than a reaction to a ticker symbol, a recent performance chart, or a familiar brand name. The first question is the most basic: what problem is this fund supposed to solve? If the answer is vague, the purchase is probably premature. An ETF should have a clear job in the portfolio, whether that job is broad market exposure, income, inflation sensitivity, a sector tilt, or a temporary implementation tool. If the fund's role cannot be stated in one sentence, it is harder to judge whether the exposure is necessary, redundant, or merely interesting.

The next question is equally important: what does the ETF actually own? A fund's name may suggest a broad category, but the holdings can reveal a much narrower or more specialized exposure. This is where investors should look past labels and examine the underlying index, sector mix, country mix, maturity profile, credit quality, or factor emphasis. Research on index investing has shown that "index" funds are not all built alike; the benchmark itself can vary substantially in construction and intent [10]. Two ETFs can both appear to offer diversification while still concentrating risk in the same industries, styles, or issuers. The holdings list is not a formality; it is the fund's real economic identity.

It is also worth asking how the ETF is built and how that structure may affect risk. Some funds hold securities directly, while others use derivatives or other synthetic methods to replicate an index. That distinction can matter for tracking behavior and for the types of risks an investor is taking on. Studies comparing physical and synthetic replication note that the two approaches differ in their sources of tracking error and in the risks embedded in the structure [61]. For a plain-vanilla investor, the practical question is not which method is universally superior, but whether the method fits the exposure being sought and whether any added complexity is justified by the fund's objective.

Another useful question is how well does the ETF behave when it is not being marketed? Many investors focus on the expense ratio and overlook the trading experience. A fund with a low published fee can still be costly if the spread is wide, the underlying market is thin, or the ETF trades at a persistent premium or discount. Liquidity should be considered at both the share level and the portfolio level. A highly traded ETF can still be harder to use efficiently if its holdings are illiquid or if the market is stressed. The investor should ask not only whether the ETF is cheap, but whether it is cheap to own and cheap to trade in realistic conditions.

A fifth question is how transparent is the fund's process? Transparency is not merely a disclosure virtue; it affects how confidently an investor can evaluate what is being held, why it is being held, and how often it changes. Modern disclosure has become one of the central mechanisms through which markets discipline fund behavior, particularly in areas where investors rely on product descriptions to make choices [4]. For ETFs, that means reviewing the index methodology, rebalancing schedule, turnover, and any screening rules that may quietly alter the risk profile. A strategy can sound straightforward while still relying on a complex selection process that changes its exposures in ways a buyer may not expect.

It is also sensible to ask who stands behind the fund and how long the strategy has been in place. Sponsor reputation is not a guarantee, but it can indicate how much operational discipline, product support, and oversight an investor is likely to receive. A long-running fund with stable methodology offers more evidence than a new launch with a compelling theme but little market history. This matters because ETF product design has become increasingly varied, and the market now includes many funds that are active in practice even when they are marketed as passive or rules-based [2]. The label on the package should not substitute for evidence about how the package is managed.

Finally, ask how the ETF fits with the rest of the portfolio and whether it creates hidden overlap. A new purchase should not be evaluated in isolation. It should be checked against existing holdings for duplication, unintended concentration, and factor crowding. This is especially important when several funds are being used to build what appears to be a diversified portfolio. Multiple ETFs can create the illusion of breadth while still pointing to the same underlying return drivers. The investor should be able to explain, before buying, what new exposure is being added, what existing exposure is being reduced, and whether the combination still matches the intended risk level. In practice, that means asking a final set of questions before placing the order:

What exact role will this ETF play in the portfolio?

What does it hold, and what exposures does that create?

How is it constructed, and does the structure add complexity or risk?

What are the all-in costs, including trading friction?

How transparent is the methodology and how often does it change?

Does it overlap with holdings I already own?

Is the fund's design consistent with my time horizon and risk tolerance?

Those questions do not eliminate uncertainty, but they force the purchase to be evaluated as a portfolio decision rather than a product impulse. That shift is what keeps ETF investing disciplined: the fund is not chosen because it is available, but because it answers a specific need better than the alternatives.

www.ingramcontent.com/pod-product-compliance
Lightning Source LLC
LaVergne TN
LVHW040519210926
848480LV00007BA/1520
9781764711180